# Collins

**Chemistry**

# AQA GCSE

# Chemistry

## Foundation

Foundation

AQA GCSE 9-1

Practice test papers

Practice test papers

2 x tests

Sunetra Berry and Paul Lewis

# Contents

## SET A

## SET B

# Acknowledgements

The authors and publisher are grateful to the copyright holders for permission to use quoted materials and images.

All images are © HarperCollins*Publishers* and Shutterstock.com

Every effort has been made to trace copyright holders and obtain their permission for the use of copyright material. The author and publisher will gladly receive information enabling them to rectify any error or omission in subsequent editions. All facts are correct at time of going to press.

Published by Collins
An imprint of HarperCollins*Publishers*
1 London Bridge Street
London SE1 9GF

© HarperCollins*Publishers* Limited 2019

ISBN 9780008321420

First published 2019

10 9 8 7 6 5 4 3 2

All rights reserved. No part of this publication may be reproduced, stored in a retrieval system, or transmitted, in any form or by any means, electronic, mechanical, photocopying, recording or otherwise, without the prior permission of Collins.

British Library Cataloguing in Publication Data.

A CIP record of this book is available from the British Library.

Commissioning Editor: Kerry Ferguson
Project Leader and Management: Chantal Addy and Shelley Teasdale
Authors: Sunetra Berry and Paul Lewis
Cover Design: Sarah Duxbury
Inside Concept Design: Ian Wrigley
Text Design and Layout: QBS Learning
Production: Karen Nulty

Printed and bound by CPI Group (UK) Ltd, Croydon, CR0 4YY

**MIX**
Paper from responsible source
FSC www.fsc.org **FSC™ C007454**

This book is produced from independently certified FSC™ paper to ensure responsible forest management.

For more information visit:
www.harpercollins.co.uk/green

©HarperCollins*Publishers* 2019

# Collins

# AQA

GCSE

# Chemistry

**F**

## SET A – Paper 1 Foundation Tier

Author: Sunetra Berry

**Materials**                                        Time allowed: 1 hour 45 minutes

**For this paper you must have:**

- a ruler
- a calculator
- the Periodic Table (found on page 94).

## Instructions

- Answer all questions in the spaces provided.
- Do all rough work in this book. Cross through any work you do not want to be marked.

## Information

- There are 100 marks available on this paper.
- The marks for questions are shown in brackets.
- You are expected to use a calculator where appropriate.
- You are reminded of the need for good English and clear presentation in your answers.
- When answering questions 02.2 and 06.3 you need to make sure that your answer:
  - is clear, logical, sensibly structured
  - fully meets the requirements of the question
  - shows that each separate point or step supports the overall answer.

## Advice

- In all calculations, show clearly how you work out your answer.

**Name:** ................................................................................................................

**01** This question is about the Periodic Table.

**01.1** Which of the statements below is **true**?

Tick **one** box.

Columns in the Periodic Table are known as periods. ☐

Rows in the Periodic Table are known as groups. ☐

The top right corner contains non-metals only. ☐

The first column contains transition metals only. ☐

[1 mark]

**01.2** Complete the sentence below.

Tick **one** box.

Noble gases are unreactive because they…

are covalently bonded molecules ☐

have low melting points ☐

are gases at room temperature ☐

have a full outer shell of electrons ☐

[1 mark]

**01.3** Which of the statements below are **true**?

Tick **two** boxes.

Group 7 elements have seven electrons in the outer most shell. ☐

Group 7 elements have very high melting and boiling points. ☐

Group 7 elements conduct electricity as liquids and gases. ☐

Group 7 elements form both ionic compounds and covalent molecules. ☐

[2 marks]

©HarperCollins*Publishers* 2019

**01.4** Describe how the reactivity of Group 1 elements changes as you look down the group in the Periodic Table.

....................................................................................................................................

....................................................................................................................................
**[1 mark]**

**01.5** Describe how the reactivity of Group 7 elements changes as you look down the group in the Periodic Table.

....................................................................................................................................

....................................................................................................................................
**[1 mark]**

**01.6** Describe how the boiling points of Group 0 elements change as you look down the group in the Periodic Table.

....................................................................................................................................

....................................................................................................................................
**[1 mark]**

**01.7** Give **two** ways in which the physical properties of transition metals **differ** from Group 1 metals.

1. ................................................................................................................................

2. ................................................................................................................................
**[2 marks]**

**Turn over >**

**02**  Magnesium oxide reacts with sulfuric acid to make a salt.

**02.1** What is the name of the **salt** that is formed?

......................................................................................................................................
[1 mark]

**02.2** Describe a method to make magnesium sulfate from insoluble magnesium oxide and sulfuric acid.

......................................................................................................................................

......................................................................................................................................

......................................................................................................................................

......................................................................................................................................

......................................................................................................................................

......................................................................................................................................

......................................................................................................................................

......................................................................................................................................

[6 marks]

**02.3** Magnesium also reacts with sulfuric acid to make the **same** salt.

What would you expect to **see** when magnesium reacts with sulfuric acid?

......................................................................................................................................

......................................................................................................................................
[1 mark]

©HarperCollins*Publishers* 2019

**02.4** Some students wanted to measure the temperature change in the reaction between magnesium and sulfuric acid.

Which of the following methods might provide them with the data they need?

Tick **one** box.

Measure the initial volume of gas and final volume of gas, using a gas syringe. ☐

Measure the initial mass and the final mass, using a balance. ☐

Measure the initial and maximum temperature of the sulfuric acid, using a thermometer. ☐

Measure the initial acidity of the sulfuric acid, using an indicator and a pH scale. ☐

**[1 mark]**

**02.5** The students repeated the method using a range of other metals.

In each case, the temperature increased, though not by the same amount.

**Table 2.1** shows the students' results.

**Table 2.1**

| Metal | Temperature change (°C) |
|---|---|
| zinc | 9 |
| copper | 3 |
| magnesium | 50 |
| iron | 5 |

Use the results to write the metals in order of reactivity, from most to least reactive.

1. ..............................................

2. ..............................................

3. ..............................................

4. ..............................................

**[2 marks]**

**03**  This question is about **nanoparticles**.

**03.1**  Which of the following statements about nanostructures are **true**?

Tick **one** box.

Nanoparticles have a low surface area to volume ratio.  ☐

Nanoparticles have a diameter less than 2500 nm.  ☐

Nanoparticles have a diameter larger than 2500 nm.  ☐

Nanoparticles have a diameter less than 1 nm.  ☐

**[1 mark]**

**03.2**  Which of the following is **not** likely to be a potential application of nanoparticles?

Tick **one** box.

New deodorants  ☐

New catalysts  ☐

New computers  ☐

New jewellery  ☐

**[1 mark]**

**03.3** Draw one line from each substance to its structure.

| Substance | Structure |
|---|---|
| buckminsterfullerene | |
| diamond | |
| graphite | |
| graphene | |

[3 marks]

**03.4** Which **two** of the following statements apply to **all** the structures in question 03.3?

Tick **two** boxes.

The atoms are joined by ionic bonds. ☐

They are made from carbon atoms only. ☐

The atoms are joined by covalent bonds. ☐

They conduct electricity. ☐

[2 marks]

**Question 3 continues on the next page**

**03.5** Write down **three** properties that are shown by both ionic compounds **and** metals.

1. ........................................................................................................

2. ........................................................................................................

3. ........................................................................................................ **[3 marks]**

**03.6** State **three similarities** and **two differences** between graphite and diamond in terms of their bonding and structures.

...........................................................................................................

...........................................................................................................

...........................................................................................................

...........................................................................................................

...........................................................................................................

...........................................................................................................

...........................................................................................................

...........................................................................................................

**[5 marks]**

©HarperCollins*Publishers* 2019

**04**   Sodium oxide is formed when sodium metal reacts with oxygen.

**04.1**  Write a word equation for the reaction.

.................................................................................................................... **[1 mark]**

**04.2**  What **type of reaction is this?**

Reduction ☐

Oxidation ☐

Neutralisation ☐

Displacement ☐                                              **[1 mark]**

**04.3**  Describe how the mass of sodium changes during the reaction.

.................................................................................................................... **[1 mark]**

**04.4**  Sodium atoms transfer electrons and form sodium ions.

Oxygen atoms accept electrons and form oxide ions.

Explain why the formula of sodium oxide is $Na_2O$

....................................................................................................................

....................................................................................................................

....................................................................................................................

....................................................................................................................

....................................................................................................................

....................................................................................................................

....................................................................................................................

                                                                  **[4 marks]**

**Question 4 continues on the next page**

**04.5** Complete the **balanced** symbol equation for the reaction.

$$\text{\_\_\_\_ Na} + O_2 \rightarrow \text{\_\_\_\_ Na}_2O$$

**[1 mark]**

**04.6** Manufacturers calculate that theoretically they might obtain 62.0 tonnes of sodium oxide from 46.0 tonnes of sodium.

They **actually** obtain 55.0 tonnes of sodium oxide.

Calculate the percentage yield.

Percentage yield = _____ %    **[1 mark]**

**04.7** The percentage atom economy of a reaction is calculated using the balanced equation for the reaction as follows:

$$\frac{\text{Relative formula mass of desired product from equation}}{\text{Sum of relative formula mass of all reactants from equation}} \times 100$$

What is the atom economy for the reaction to make sodium oxide?

Give a reason for your answer.

Percentage atom economy: _____

Reason: _____

_____    **[2 marks]**

**04.8** Sodium oxide can also be made by the thermal decomposition of sodium carbonate.

The other product is carbon dioxide.

Write a **balanced** symbol equation for this reaction.

_____ **[1 mark]**

**04.9** How would you expect the mass of the solid sodium carbonate to have changed after this reaction is complete?

_____ **[1 mark]**

**04.10** How is the atom economy different in this reaction compared to the reaction in 04.5?

Explain your answer.

_____

_____

_____

_____ **[2 marks]**

**Turn over >**

05  A student wanted to find out if reactions were exothermic or endothermic.

They carried out four different reactions and measured the temperature changes.

They repeated each reaction three times.

**Table 5.1** shows the results.

**Table 5.1**

| Reaction | Temperature change (°C) | | | Mean temperature change (°C) |
|---|---|---|---|---|
| | Exp 1 | Exp 2 | Exp 3 | |
| A | 5 | 10 | 11 | |
| B | −5 | −6 | −6 | |
| C | 25 | 19 | 26 | |
| D | −10 | −12 | −11 | |

05.1  Calculate the mean temperature change for each reaction, to 3 significant figures.

Omit any anomalous results.

Add your answers to **Table 5.1**

[4 marks]

05.2  Are the anomalous results caused by random **or** systematic error?

Explain your answer.

......................................................................................................................

......................................................................................................................

......................................................................................................................

......................................................................................................................  [2 marks]

                    ©HarperCollins*Publishers* 2019

**05.3** Give **three** conclusions about the four reactions that you can draw from this data.

.......................................................................................................................................

.......................................................................................................................................

.......................................................................................................................................

.......................................................................................................................................

.......................................................................................................................................

.......................................................................................................................................  **[3 marks]**

**05.4** Match each of the four reactions, A, B, C and D, to one of the energy profiles in **Figure 5.1**

**Figure 5.1**

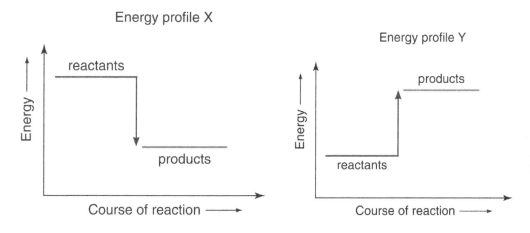

| Reaction | Energy profile (X or Y) |
|----------|-------------------------|
| A        |                         |
| B        |                         |
| C        |                         |
| D        |                         |

**[2 marks]**

**Turn over >**

**06**   A student carries out a titration between 25 cm³ potassium hydroxide and nitric acid.

**06.1** What are the names of the products formed?

_____ **[1 mark]**

**06.2** The concentration of potassium hydroxide needs to be 10 g/dm³

Calculate the amount of potassium hydroxide that needs to be dissolved to make 25 cm³ of solution.

_____

_____

Amount of potassium hydroxide = _____ g  **[2 marks]**

**06.3** Describe how to carry out the titration.

Include any chemicals and equipment needed.

_____

_____

_____

_____

_____

_____

_____

_____

_____

**[6 marks]**

©HarperCollins*Publishers* 2019

**07**  Some students investigated the temperature during the neutralisation of sodium hydroxide and hydrochloric acid.

The students used the apparatus in **Figure 7.1** to collect the data.

**Figure 7.1**

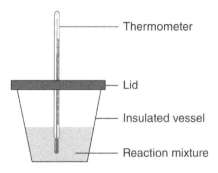

The students carried out eight experiments. In each experiment, they added a volume of 2 mol/dm³ sodium hydroxide to a fixed volume and concentration of hydrochloric acid.

The volumes of 2 mol/dm³ sodium hydroxide added and the temperatures recorded are shown in **Table 7.1**

**Table 7.1**

| Volume of NaOH (cm³) | Temperature (°C) |
|---|---|
| 5 | 25.80 |
| 10 | 26.40 |
| 15 | 27.00 |
| 20 | 27.60 |
| 25 | 27.40 |
| 30 | 27.20 |
| 35 | 27.00 |
| 40 | 26.80 |

**07.1**  Name a suitable material to make the insulating material and the lid in **Figure 7.1**

[1 mark]

_____

**Question 7 continues on the next page**

**07.2** Using a suitable scale on your axes, plot **all** the points from **Table 7.1** on the grid below.

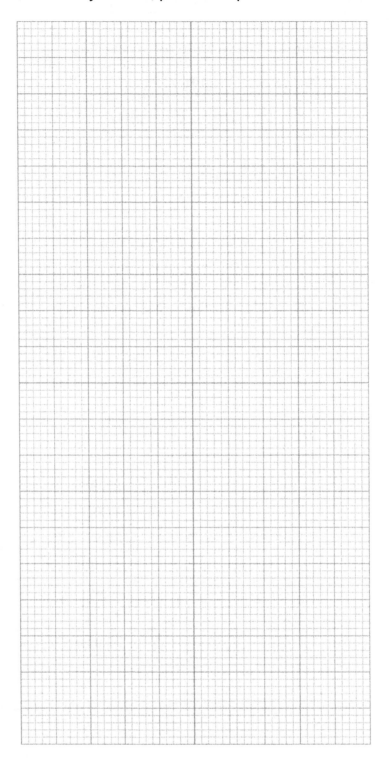

[4 marks]

©HarperCollins*Publishers* 2019

**07.3** Draw two straight lines of best fit on the graph to show how the temperature changes as the volume increases.

**[2 marks]**

**07.4** The **point of neutralisation** occurs at the highest temperature rise.

What is the volume of sodium hydroxide at the point of neutralisation?

**[1 mark]**

**07.5** Add state symbols to complete the equation for this reaction.

$H^+$ ( ............... ) + $OH^-$ ( ............... ) → $H_2O$ ( ............... )          **[1 mark]**

**07.6** Draw **one** line from each volume of sodium hydroxide added to the acid to the acid's expected pH range.

Volume of sodium
hydroxide (cm³)                                          pH range

                                                        | 0–2 |

| 10 |                                                  | 2–4 |

| 25 |                                                  | 4–6 |

| 40 |                                                  | 6–8 |

| 15 |                                                  | 8–10 |

                                                        | 10–12 |

**[4 marks]**

**08.1** Which diagram represents the correct atomic structure for oxygen?

$$^{16}_{8}O$$

Tick **one** box.

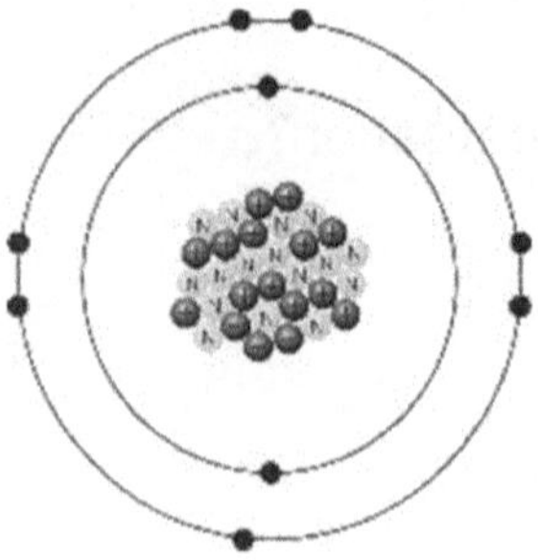

☐

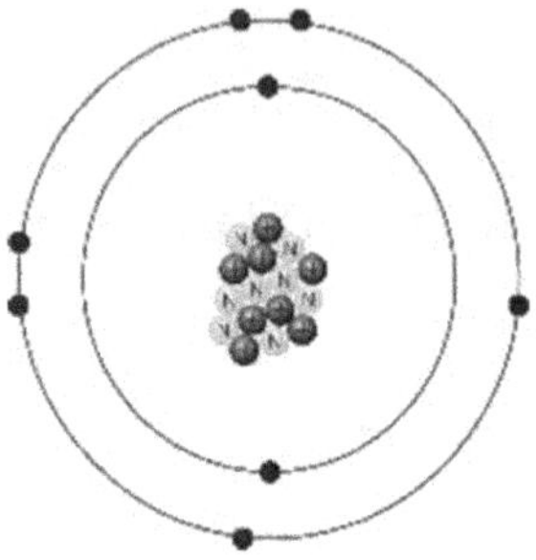

☐

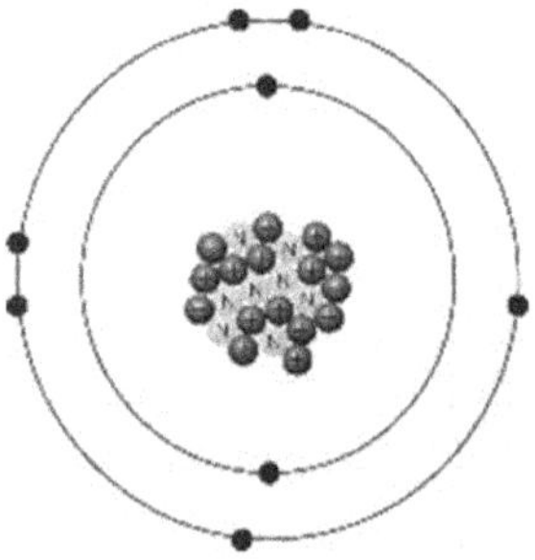

☐

[1 mark]

**08.2** Draw the electronic structure of the **oxide ion.**

[2 marks]

**08.3** Which statement about the sizes of the atoms and the nucleus is true?

Tick **one** box.

The radius of an atom is about 10 nm ☐

The radius of a nucleus is about 10 nm ☐

The radius of an atom is about 0.1 nm ☐

The radius of a nucleus is about 0.1 nm ☐

**[1 mark]**

**08.4** Which **two** statements about isotopes are true?

Tick **two** boxes.

Isotopes have the same physical properties. ☐

Isotopes contain the same number of protons. ☐

Isotopes contain the same number of neutrons. ☐

Isotopes contain the same number of electrons. ☐

**[2 marks]**

**08.5** Oxygen has three isotopes:

$$^{16}_{8}O \qquad ^{17}_{8}O \qquad ^{18}_{8}O$$

Describe the **similarities** and **differences** between the three isotopes of oxygen.

........................................................................................................

........................................................................................................

........................................................................................................

........................................................................................................

**[2 marks]**

**Question 8 continues on the next page**

**08.6** **Table 8.1** shows the percentage of each isotope in a sample of oxygen.

**Table 8.1**

| Percentage | Isotope |
|---|---|
| 70 | $^{16}_{8}O$ |
| 25 | $^{17}_{8}O$ |
| 5 | $^{18}_{8}O$ |

Calculate the relative atomic mass of oxygen in the sample.

Give your answer to 4 significant figures.

............................................................................................................................

............................................................................................................................

............................................................................................................................

............................................................................................................................

............................................................................................................................

**[3 marks]**

**09** Scientists used to think that atoms were like 'plum puddings'. An experiment using positively charged alpha particles and gold foil changed scientists' ideas.

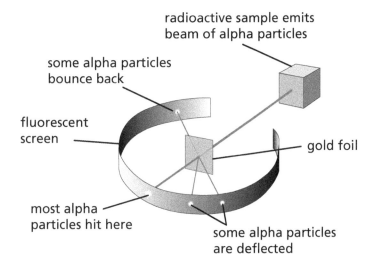

1. Scientists thought the alpha particles would pass straight through the gold foil.
2. Alpha particles were fired at a sheet of gold foil.
3. Some alpha particles did go straight through the gold foil; others were deflected.

**09.1** Which **two** statements about Rutherford's experiment **provided evidence** for the nuclear model of the atom?

Tick **two** boxes.

The beam produced is deflected by an electric field. ☐

Alpha particles were fired at a thin piece of gold foil. ☐

A high voltage was applied to produce a beam. ☐

Flashes of light were observed when particles hit a screen. ☐   **[2 marks]**

**09.2** Describe the evidence collected through this experiment.

Explain how the evidence led to new conclusions about the structure of the atom.

**[4 marks]**

**END OF QUESTIONS**

**BLANK PAGE**

©HarperCollins*Publishers* 2019

# Collins

# AQA

GCSE

# Chemistry

**F**

## SET A – Paper 2 Foundation Tier

Author: Sunetra Berry

**Materials**

Time allowed: 1 hour 45 minutes

**For this paper you must have:**

- a ruler
- a calculator
- the Periodic Table (found on page 94).

**Instructions**

- Answer all questions in the spaces provided.
- Do all rough work in this book. Cross through any work you do not want to be marked.

**Information**

- There are 100 marks available on this paper.
- The marks for questions are shown in brackets.
- You are expected to use a calculator where appropriate.
- You are reminded of the need for good English and clear presentation in your answers.
- When answering question 07.5 you need to make sure that your answer:
  - is clear, logical, sensibly structured
  - fully meets the requirements of the question
  - shows that each separate point or step supports the overall answer.

**Advice**

- In all calculations, show clearly how you work out your answer.

**Name:** ................................................................................................

**01.1** Which **one** of the following substances is pure?

Tick **one** box.

Air in a city ☐

Sea water near a factory ☐

Oxygen from a cylinder ☐

Chocolate milkshake ☐

**[1 mark]**

**01.2** Which statement about pure substances is **false**?

Tick **one** box.

A pure substance can be an element or a compound. ☐

Formulations must be pure substances in order to be safe. ☐

Pure substances have specific melting points and boiling points. ☐

A mixture can be pure. ☐

**[1 mark]**

©HarperCollins*Publishers* 2019

**01.3** Identify the following substances as mixtures or formulations.

Write either M (for mixture) or F (for formulation) in **each** row in **Table 1.1**

Table 1.1

| Name of substance | Formulation or mixture |
|---|---|
| baby food | |
| rock salt and sand | |
| cough medicine | |
| sea water | |

[4 marks]

**01.4** Which **one** of the following gases is **not** considered to be an atmospheric pollutant produced by the combustion of fuels?

Tick **one** box.

Sulfur dioxide ☐

Carbon monoxide ☐

Oxides of nitrogen ☐

Oxygen ☐

[1 mark]

**01.5** Name the two main greenhouse gases.

Greenhouse gas 1. _____

Greenhouse gas 2. _____ [2 marks]

Turn over >

**02.1** Which list shows the first four members of the **alkanes** in the correct order?

Tick **one** box.

Ethene, propene, butane, pentene ☐

Methane, ethane, propane, butane ☐

Butane, ethane, methane, propane ☐

Butene, ethene, pentene, propene ☐

**[1 mark]**

**02.2** Which statement about alkanes **and** alkenes is **true**?

Tick **one** box.

Alkanes and alkenes are both part of a homologous series. ☐

The general formula for alkanes is $C_nH_{2n}$ and for alkenes is $C_nH_{2n+2}$ ☐

Alkenes are saturated hydrocarbons and alkanes are unsaturated. ☐

Alkanes contain a double bond between C atoms and alkenes don't. ☐

**[1 mark]**

**02.3** Tick **two** boxes that correctly complete the sentence below.

As the size of alkane and alkene molecules **increases**…

…they burn more readily and more completely. ☐

…they can flow less easily and are harder to pour. ☐

…the boiling point increases. ☐

…the flammability increases. ☐

**[2 marks]**

**02.4** Which of the following is an **alkene**?

Tick **one** box.

H—C—C—H (ethane structure) ☐

H—C—C—C—C—O—H (butanol structure) ☐

C=C—C—H (propene structure) ☐

H—C—C—C (propanoic acid structure) ☐

[1 mark]

**02.5** Complete the following sentences about **fractional distillation**.

Use the correct words from the grid.

| compound | melting | cool | mixture | boiling |
|----------|---------|------|---------|---------|
| melt | evaporate | freeze | condense | solidify |

Crude oil is a _____ of hydrocarbons.

This means it can be separated into fractions.

The fractions have different _____ points.

Heating the crude oil causes the fractions to _____ .

As they move up the fractionating column, they _____
and _____ .

[5 marks]

Turn over >

**03.1** Which statement about the reactions of organic molecules is **false**?

Tick **one** box.

Alkanes and alkenes are both very reactive. ☐

Ethanol and ethane burn to make carbon dioxide and water. ☐

Hydrogen and halogens can be added to alkenes. ☐

Ethanoic acid reacts with carbonates to make carbon dioxide. ☐

**[1 mark]**

**03.2** What is the product when hydrogen reacts with propene?

Tick **one** box.

Propanol ☐

Propanoic acid ☐

Propyl propanoate ☐

Propane ☐

**[1 mark]**

**03.3** Which **two** statements about cracking are true?

Tick **two** boxes.

Steam cracking takes place at a higher temperature than catalytic cracking. ☐

More alkenes are produced in steam cracking than catalytic cracking. ☐

More alkenes are produced in catalytic cracking than steam cracking. ☐

Steam cracking and catalytic cracking require high operating pressures. ☐

**[2 marks]**

©HarperCollins*Publishers* 2019

**03.4** Describe the test that can show whether a substance is propane or propene.

Include the expected results for each substance.

Test ..........................................................................................................................

Expected results .......................................................................................

............................................................................................................................ **[2 marks]**

**03.5** Complete the symbol equation for the cracking of dodecane ($C_{12}H_{26}$).

$$C_{12}H_{26} \rightarrow C_3H_6 + C_4H_8 + C_{\phantom{.}}H_{\phantom{.}}$$

**[2 marks]**

**03.6** Ethanol can be manufactured by reacting steam ($H_2O$) with a hydrocarbon.

What is the name of the hydrocarbon?

.......................................................................................................................... **[1 mark]**

**03.7** Ethanol can also be produced by fermentation of sugar solution.

Draw **two** lines from **each** process to the **two** conditions required to carry it out.

**Process**                               **Condition**

| high temperature and pressure |

| fermentation |

| low temperature and pressure |

| adding water to a hydrocarbon |

| anaerobic |

| addition of a metal catalyst |

**[2 marks]**

**04.1** Which **one** of the following statements about the factors affecting the rate of reaction is **true**?

Tick **one** box.

The rate of reaction is faster with a lower temperature.  ☐

The rate of reaction is faster with a higher concentration.  ☐

The rate of reaction is slower with a catalyst.  ☐

The rate of reaction is faster with a lower pressure.  ☐

**[1 mark]**

**04.2** Which one of the following is **not** a unit for rate of reaction?

Tick **one** box.

g/s  ☐

$cm^3$/s  ☐

kg/hr  ☐

m/s  ☐

**[1 mark]**

©HarperCollins*Publishers* 2019

**04.3** A student investigated the rate of the following reaction:

magnesium + hydrochloric acid → magnesium chloride + hydrogen

The student used apparatus as shown in **Figure 4.1**

**Figure 4.1**

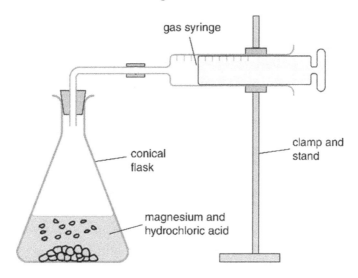

How could the mean rate of reaction of the complete reaction be measured most accurately?

Tick **one** box.

Measure the total volume of hydrogen in the gas syringe
and divide by the time taken to make it.                                    ☐

Measure the time taken for the bubbles of hydrogen
to stop being made.                                                        ☐

Measure the time taken for the magnesium to completely
react and dissolve.                                                        ☐

Measure the time taken for 10 cm³ of hydrogen to be made,
and divide by the time taken to make the 10 cm³ of hydrogen.               ☐

[1 mark]

**Question 4 continues on the next page**

**04.4** The rate of reaction was measured for different concentrations of acid.

**Table 4.1** shows the results.

**Table 4.1**

| Time for the reaction to complete (s) | Concentration of acid (g / dm³) |
|---|---|
| 120 | 0.5 |
| 100 | 1.0 |
| 50 | 1.5 |
| 25 | 2.0 |
| 18 | 2.5 |
| 15 | 3.0 |

On the grid below:

• Plot these results

• Draw a line of best fit

• Highlight any anomalous points

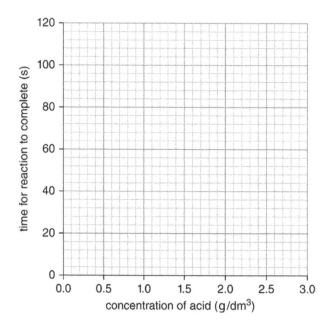

**[3 marks]**

©HarperCollins*Publishers* 2019

**04.5** The total volume of hydrogen produced in each reaction was 900 cm³

Calculate the rate of reaction at the **highest** concentration in **Table 4.1**

Use the equation:

$$\text{mean rate of reaction} = \frac{\text{total volume of hydrogen made (cm}^3)}{\text{time taken (s)}}$$

Mean rate of reaction = _____ cm³/s   **[2 marks]**

**04.6** Describe how the rate of reaction changes with concentration.

Use the data in **Table 4.1** and/or your graph.

_____ **[1 mark]**

**04.7** Explain why the rate changes with increasing concentration.

Use your knowledge of particles and collisions.

_____

_____

_____

_____

_____ **[2 marks]**

**Turn over >**

**05.1** Draw **one** line from each gas to the test used to identify it.

Gas | Test and result

bubble gas through limewater; limewater will turn cloudy

hydrogen

its volume at 100 °C is less than its volume at 20 °C

chlorine

insert glowing splint; splint will relight

oxygen

conducts electricity

carbon dioxide

place damp litmus into the gas; litmus will turn white

insert burning splint; a pop sound is heard

[4 marks]

**05.2** An unknown metal salt was added to sodium hydroxide solution.

A blue precipitate was observed.

The unknown metal salt produced a green flame.

Name the metal ion in the unknown metal salt.

Include its charge.

.................................................................................................................................... [1 mark]

**05.3** The unknown metal salt is a sulfate.

Describe a suitable test to show whether sulfate ions are present.

Include the expected result if sulfate ions are present.

Test ...............................................................................................................................

....................................................................................................................................

Expected result ..................................................................................... [2 marks]

©HarperCollins*Publishers* 2019

**05.4** **Table 5.1** shows the results of tests on two salts.

**Table 5.1**

| Salt | Test and result | | | |
|------|------------|---------------------------------|--------------------------------|---------------------------------|
|  | **Flame test** | **Add acidified barium chloride** | **Add acidified silver nitrate** | **Add sodium hydroxide solution** |
| A | crimson flame | no change | cream precipitate | no result |
| B | unclear | white precipitate | no result | brown precipitate |

Analyse and interpret the results to identify the cations (metal ions) and anions (non-metal ions) in each salt.

Cation in salt A .......................................................................................................................

Anion in salt A .......................................................................................................................

Cation in salt B .......................................................................................................................

Anion in salt B ................................................................................................... **[4 marks]**

**05.5** Give three reasons why **instrumental** methods of chemical detection are preferred to **chemical** methods.

.................................................................................................................................................

.................................................................................................................................................

.................................................................................................................................................

.................................................................................................................................................

.................................................................................................................................................

.................................................................................................................... **[3 marks]**

**Question 5 continues on the next page**

05.6 Flame emission spectroscopy can be used to analyse metal ions in solution.

Figure 5.1 shows the results from a flame emission analysis of different elements.

**Figure 5.1**

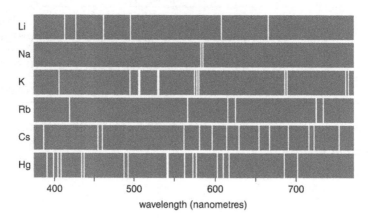

An unknown salt was analysed using flame emission spectroscopy.

The result for the salt is shown in **Figure 5.2**

**Figure 5.2**

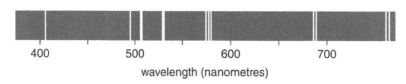

Compare **Figure 5.1** and **Figure 5.2**

What conclusion can you draw?

Explain your answer.

......................................................................................................................................................................

...................................................................................................................................................... **[2 marks]**

©HarperCollins*Publishers* 2019

06    **Table 6.1** shows the composition of gases in the early atmosphere and the composition of gases in the atmosphere today.

Table 6.1

| Name of gas | Composition in early atmosphere (%) | Composition in atmosphere today (%) |
|---|---|---|
| carbon dioxide | 98 | 0.04 |
| oxygen | 0 | 20 |
| nitrogen | 0 | 80 |
| ammonia | small amounts | none |
| methane | small amounts | small amounts |
| water | variable | variable |

06.1  Describe **three** differences between the gases in the early atmosphere and the gases in the atmosphere today.

_____

_____

_____

_____

_____

**[3 marks]**

**Question 6 continues on the next page**

**06.2** Carbon dioxide levels have changed between the early atmosphere and the present atmosphere.

Describe **two** different processes that account for these changes.

Explain why each of them has caused the change.

_____

_____

_____

_____

_____ **[4 marks]**

**06.3** Oxygen in the atmosphere is produced by only one process.

Write a balanced symbol equation for this process.

_____ **[2 marks]**

**06.4** Describe **two** of the effects of the recent increase in average global temperature.

_____

_____

_____ **[2 marks]**

©HarperCollins*Publishers* 2019

**06.5** Describe **four** possible actions that could be taken to reduce the emissions of greenhouse gases.

Explain why each of these actions would lead to a reduction.

[4 marks]

**07.1** What is the difference between **potable** water and **pure** water?

........................................................................................................................

........................................................................................................................ **[1 mark]**

**07.2** Two rivers, A and B, were considered as possible sources of drinking water.

Water samples from both rivers were analysed to test if they were potable.

The data from both rivers are given in **Table 7.1**, alongside data for recommended safe drinking water quality.

Table 7.1

| | | Maximum recommended level | River A | River B |
|---|---|---|---|---|
| | hardness | 1500 mg/l | 1000 mg/l | 3000 mg/l |
| Ion concentration (mg/l) | chloride | 500 | 12 800 | 500 |
| | sulfate | 1000 | 1 | 1 |
| | iron | 50 | 20 | 30 |
| | magnesium | 200 | 150 | 150 |
| | sodium | 500 | 3000 | 500 |
| | nitrate | 50 | 20 | 20 |
| | pH value | 6.0–8.5 | 5.5 | 7.0 |

Which of the two rivers would be most appropriate to use as a source for potential potable water?

Give **three** reasons for your answer.

Use the data in **Table 7.1**

River ..............................................................

Reasons ..............................................................................................

........................................................................................................................

........................................................................................................................

........................................................................................................................

........................................................................................................................

........................................................................................................................

........................................................................................................................ **[4 marks]**

©HarperCollins*Publishers* 2019

**07.3** What are the **two** water treatment processes used to treat water from **all** potential water sources?

_____

_____

_____ **[2 marks]**

**07.4** Explain why ozone may be added to produce potable water.

_____

_____

_____ **[2 marks]**

**Question 7 continues on the next page**

**07.5** Potable water can be produced either from seawater or from groundwater.

Compare the similarities and differences in the processes involved to obtain potable water from each of these sources.

......................................................................................................................................

......................................................................................................................................

......................................................................................................................................

......................................................................................................................................

......................................................................................................................................

......................................................................................................................................

......................................................................................................................................

......................................................................................................................................

......................................................................................................................................

...................................................................................................................... **[6 marks]**

©HarperCollins*Publishers* 2019

08   Ammonia is produced using this reaction:

nitrogen + hydrogen ⇌ ammonia

08.1  What does the ⇌ sign mean?

_____  [1 mark]

08.2  If the reaction is exothermic in the forward direction, what can you say about the reverse direction?

_____  [1 mark]

08.3  Describe the conditions used industrially for the reaction above.

_____

_____

_____

[3 marks]

08.4  NPK fertilisers are produced from different raw materials.

Name the **two** substances that are needed to make **ammonium phosphate** using a neutralisation reaction.

_____

_____

[2 marks]

**Question 8 continues on the next page**

**08.5** NPK fertilisers are formulations of various salts containing appropriate percentages of the elements.

The salts contain three important elements.

State the names of these elements.

[2 marks]

**08.6** Phosphate rock contains calcium phosphate.

When treated with nitric acid the products are a weak acid and a salt of a strong acid.

The weak acid is reacted with ammonium hydroxide to produce ammonium phosphate, a soluble salt that is used as a fertiliser.

Write two word equations to show these two reactions which lead to the production of ammonium phosphate.

[4 marks]

**END OF QUESTIONS**

 ©HarperCollins*Publishers* 2019

# Collins

# AQA

GCSE

# Chemistry

F

## SET B – Paper 1 Foundation Tier

Author: Paul Lewis

**Materials**

Time allowed: 1 hour 45 minutes

**For this paper you must have:**

- a ruler
- a calculator
- the Periodic Table (found on page 94).

## Instructions

- Answer **all** questions in the spaces provided.
- Do all rough work in this book. Cross through any work you do not want to be marked.

## Information

- There are 100 marks available on this paper.
- The marks for questions are shown in brackets.
- You are expected to use a calculator where appropriate.
- You are reminded of the need for good English and clear presentation in your answers.
- When answering questions 07.6 and 10.4 you need to make sure that your answer:
  - is clear, logical, sensibly structured
  - fully meets the requirements of the question
  - shows that each separate point or step supports the overall answer.

## Advice

- In all calculations, show clearly how you work out your answer.

**Name:** ...........................................................................................................................

01    This question is about atomic structure and the Periodic Table.

01.1  **Figure 1.1** shows the location of some of the elements in the Periodic Table.

The letters are **not** the actual symbols for the elements in that location.

**Figure 1.1**

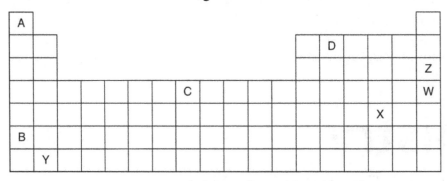

Write letters from **Figure 1.1** to identify the following.

| | |
|---|---|
| Two elements in the same period | |
| An element with a full outer shell | |
| A transition metal | |
| An element with only six protons | |

[4 marks]

01.2  Identify the correct electron configuration for nitrogen.

Tick **one** box.

2,8,6      ☐

2,7        ☐

2,5        ☐

2,2,3      ☐

[1 mark]

**01.3** How many protons are there in a nitrogen atom?

Tick **one** box.

5 ☐

7 ☐

9 ☐

14 ☐

[1 mark]

**01.4** Explain why a nitrogen atom has no overall charge.

........................................................................................................................

........................................................................................................................

........................................................................................................................

........................................................................................................................

[3 marks]

**01.5** Draw **one** line from each word to its definition.

| Word | Definition |
|------|------------|

**Word**

element

compound

mixture

**Definition**

where two or more substances are together but can be separated

a substance that is made from only one type of atom

a substance that contains only neutrons and protons

where two or more substances have chemically combined

[1 mark]

Turn over >

**02** All metals in Group 1 react in a similar way.

For example, when potassium reacts with water, the reaction can be represented by:

$$K(s) + H_2O(l) \rightarrow KOH(aq) + H_2(g)$$

**02.1** Name the **gas** produced.

[1 mark]

**02.2** Some students place 1 g of a Group 1 metal into a trough of water.

At the end of the reaction, one of the students adds a few drops of universal indicator to the trough.

The solution turns a light purple, meaning it has become alkaline.

Which **ion** makes the solution alkaline?

[1 mark]

**02.3** The reactions of **potassium with water** and **sodium with water** are similar, but not identical.

State **two** differences between the reaction of potassium and water compared to the reaction of sodium and water.

1.

2.

[2 marks]

 ©HarperCollins*Publishers* 2019

**02.4** Explain why the elements in Group 1 get more reactive further down the group when moving from lithium to francium.

_____

_____

_____

_____

_____

_____

**[3 marks]**

**02.5** Silver and gold are transition metals.

Where are silver and gold found on the Periodic Table?

_____ **[1 mark]**

**02.6** Transition metals have different properties to Group 1 metals.

Which **two** statements about the properties of transition metals are correct?

Tick **two** boxes.

They are less reactive than Group 1 metals. ☐

They have lower densities than Group 1 metals. ☐

They have higher melting points than Group 1 metals. ☐

They do not tend to form coloured compounds, unlike Group 1 metals. ☐

**[2 marks]**

**Turn over >**

03   Some students were investigating the reactivity of four different metals.

They used 1 mol/dm³ hydrochloric acid and 3 cm lengths of each metal.

When the metals react, they release hydrogen gas as gas bubbles in the test tube.

03.1   Draw **one** line from each description to the correct variable.

| Description | Variable |
|---|---|
| independent variable | number of bubbles |
| dependent variable | type of metal |
| control variable | concentration of acid used |

[2 marks]

03.2   The students then investigated the volume of hydrogen gas produced.

**Figure 3.1** shows the apparatus used.

**Figure 3.1**

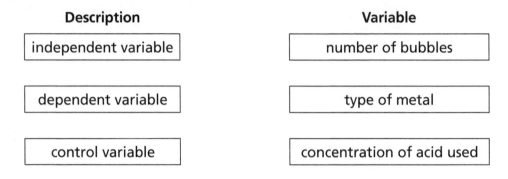

This is their method:

1. Place a 3 cm length of metal ribbon in the flask.

2. Add 15 cm³ 1 mol/dm³ hydrochloric acid.

3. Connect the piece of apparatus labelled X immediately.

4. Measure the volume of gas produced every 10 s, for a total of 60 s

What is the name of the piece of apparatus, labelled X, used to collect the hydrogen?

[1 mark]

©HarperCollins*Publishers* 2019

**03.3** Their results are shown in **Table 3.1**

**Table 3.1**

| Time (seconds) | Volume of hydrogen gas (cm³) |
|---|---|
| 0 | 0 |
| 10 | 8 |
| 20 | 16 |
| 30 | 15 |
| 40 | 21 |
| 50 | 23 |
| 60 | 23 |

Plot these results on the grid below.

Draw a line of best fit.

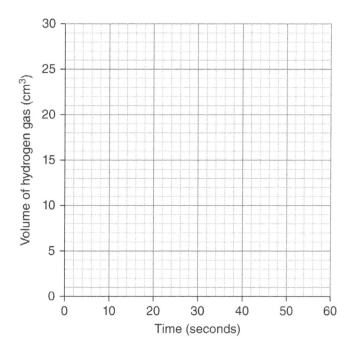

**[2 marks]**

**Question 3 continues on the next page**

**03.4** The results for magnesium have produced an anomalous result.

Identify which result is anomalous.

Explain why this result can be treated as an anomalous result.

........................................................................................................................

........................................................................................................................

........................................................................................................................ **[2 marks]**

**03.5** Describe the pattern in the results.

........................................................................................................................

........................................................................................................................

........................................................................................................................ **[2 marks]**

**03.6** The results in **Table 3.1** above show that in 50 seconds the reaction produced 23 $cm^3$ of hydrogen gas.

Calculate the mean volume of hydrogen produced per second in the reaction.

Give your answer to 1 decimal place.

........................................................................................................................

........................................................................................................................

Mean volume of hydrogen produced throughout the reaction = ........................ $cm^3$/s

**[2 marks]**

©HarperCollins*Publishers* 2019

**04**  Scientists use models as a way to show and describe what they mean.

**04.1**  Models can be used to show bonding in different structures.

Which type of structure is shown in the model of water in **Figure 4.1**?

**Figure 4.1**

H —— O —— H

Tick **one** box.

Covalent ☐

Metallic ☐

Ionic ☐

**[1 mark]**

**04.2**  Models can also be used to distinguish between different substances.

Draw **one** line from each statement to the model that shows it best.

| Statement | Model |
|-----------|-------|
| This substance is a giant covalent structure. | A  |
| This substance is a compound. | B |
| This substance is a solid. | C |
| This substance is evaporating. | D |
| This substance is a gas. | E |

**[4 marks]**

**Question 4 continues on the next page**

**04.3** **Figure 4.2** show models that different scientists have used at different times in history, to describe how the atom is structured.

**Figure 4.2**

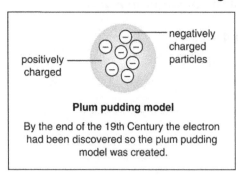

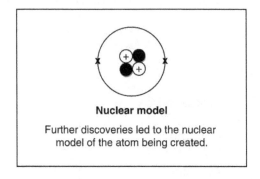

Compare the older plum pudding model with the modern nuclear model of the atom.

Use your own knowledge and the diagrams in **Figure 4.2**

......................................................................................................................................

......................................................................................................................................

......................................................................................................................................

......................................................................................................................................

......................................................................................................................................

......................................................................................................................................

......................................................................................................................................

......................................................................................................................................

**[4 marks]**

©HarperCollins*Publishers* 2019

**05** Students use the apparatus shown in **Figure 5.1** to investigate how the temperature changes as different solids dissolve.

**Figure 5.1**

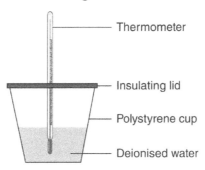

This is their method:

1. Place 25 cm³ deionised water in a polystyrene cup.

2. Measure the temperature of the water.

3. Add 1 g calcium chloride, and stir.

4. Record the highest or lowest temperature reached.

5. Repeat the experiment using potassium chloride instead of calcium chloride.

**05.1** **Table 5.1** shows the results.

**Table 5.1**

| Solute | Initial temperature in °C | Final temperature in °C |
|---|---|---|
| calcium chloride | 20 | 29 |
| potassium chloride | 20 | 14 |

Calculate the temperature change for each solute.

calcium chloride: _____ °C

potassium chloride: _____ °C                                         **[2 marks]**

**Question 5 continues on the next page**

**05.2** On the sketch graph below, draw the reaction profile for dissolving calcium chloride.

Label the reactants **and** the products on the profile.

You do not have to show activation energy.

[2 marks]

**05.3** Which of the two solutes could be used in first aid ice packs?

............................................................................................................................... [1 mark]

**05.4** What is the word used for a reaction that transfers energy **from** the reactants **to** the surroundings?

............................................................................................................................... [1 mark]

**05.5** Calcium chloride has the chemical formula $CaCl_2$

Calculate the **relative formula mass** ($M_r$) of calcium chloride.

Relative atomic masses $A_r$: Cl = 35.5; Ca = 40

...............................................................................................................................

............................................................................................................................... [1 mark]

©HarperCollins*Publishers* 2019

06.1 Choose words from the box to complete the paragraph about **metals** and **alloys**.

Use **Figure 6.1** to help you.

| hard | smooth | soft | ordered |
| harder | distorted | softer | better |

**Figure 6.1**

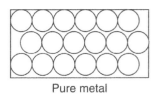 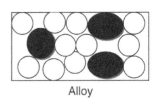

Pure metal                    Alloy

Pure metals and alloys have different properties.

A pure metal is _____, because the atoms are all arranged in layers which slide over each other.

In an alloy, the layers are _____.

This makes alloys _____ than pure metals.                    **[3 marks]**

06.2 Magnesium atoms have 12 electrons each.

Draw on **Figure 6.2** to show how the electrons are arranged in a magnesium atom.

**Figure 6.2**

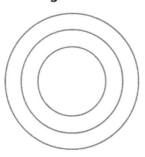

**[2 marks]**

06.3 Magnesium is in Group 2 and Period 3 of the Periodic Table.

Explain why magnesium is in this location, in terms of electrons and electron shells.

_____

_____

_____

**[2 marks]**

**Question 6 continues on the next page**

06.4 Metals have unique properties due to their chemical structure.

Draw **one** line from each property of a metal to the feature of the structure of metals.

| Property | Feature |
|---|---|
| | have layers which can slide over each other |
| good conductors of electricity | no delocalised electrons to carry a charge |
| often have a high melting point | strong covalent bonds |
| malleable | strong electrostatic forces of attraction |
| | delocalised electrons to carry a charge |

[2 marks]

06.5 Silver particles are used in plasters.

The particles have a diameter of 20 nm.

Explain, in terms of their size, why they are classed as nanoparticles.

_____ [1 mark]

06.6 A picometre is $1 \times 10^{-12}$ m

A silver atom has a radius of 165 picometres.

What is the radius of a silver atom in **nanometres**?

Give your answer in Standard Form.

_____

_____

[2 marks]

©HarperCollins*Publishers* 2019

**07**    A burette is filled to the zero line with sodium hydroxide solution.

Some of the solution is let out of the burette.

**Figure 7.1** shows the level of the remaining solution.

**Figure 7.1**

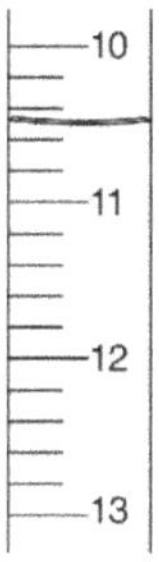

**07.1**  What is the volume of sodium hydroxide solution that was let out of the burette?

Tick **one** box.

10.25 cm³    ☐

10.50 cm³    ☐

11.50 cm³    ☐

11.25 cm³    ☐

**[1 mark]**

**07.2**  The concentration of the sodium hydroxide solution is 45 g/dm³

Calculate how many grams of sodium hydroxide there are in the sodium hydroxide solution let out of the burette.

Show your working.

_____

_____

_____ **[2 marks]**

**Question 7 continues on the next page**

**07.3** The label on the burette states ±0.25 cm³

A student uses the burette to measure 50 cm³ liquid.

What is the largest **real** volume that they could have measured?

[1 mark]

**07.4** When sodium hydroxide reacts with an acid it produces sodium sulfate.

What is the name of the acid used in the reaction?

[1 mark]

**07.5** What is the name of this **type** of reaction?

[1 mark]

©HarperCollins*Publishers* 2019

**07.6** A student will use the equipment shown in **Figure 7.2** to carry out a titration.

**Figure 7.2**

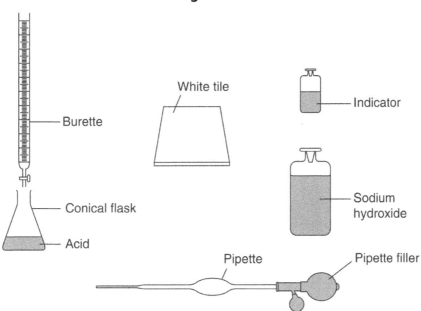

The student plans to carry out a titration to find the volume of sodium hydroxide required to react with a known volume of acid.

Describe the method they should use.

Your answer should include reference to each piece of equipment.

You do **not** need to include any calculations in your answer.

_____

_____

_____

_____

_____

_____

_____

_____

_____

_____ **[6 marks]**

**Turn over >**

08    **Figure 8.1** shows the structure of **graphene**.

**Figure 8.1**

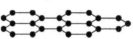

Graphene is a single layer made of the same atoms that make up graphite.

It is said that graphene:

• is the strongest material ever measured
• is one of the best conducting materials known
• may have the highest melting point in nature.

08.1  Complete the sentences about **graphene**.

Use the correct words from the boxes.

| calcium | chlorine | carbon |
|---------|----------|--------|
| three   | four     | five   |

Graphene is made from ........................................... atoms.

In graphene, each atom bonds to ........................................... other atoms.    **[2 marks]**

08.2  Graphite, like graphene, can conduct electricity.

Explain why graphite can conduct electricity.

.............................................................................................................................

.............................................................................................................................

.............................................................................................................................    **[2 marks]**

08.3  Explain why **graphite** is used in lubricants.

.............................................................................................................................

.............................................................................................................................

.............................................................................................................................    **[2 marks]**

09    Electrolysis can be used to separate some substances into their components.

09.1  Which **two** of the following substances could be separated into their components using electrolysis?

Tick **two** boxes.

Solid carbon dioxide ☐

Molten magnesium chloride ☐

A solution of potassium iodide ☐

Molten sulfur dioxide ☐

Solid potassium iodide ☐

[1 mark]

09.2  The electrolysis of sodium chloride solution (brine) can be carried out in a school laboratory or on a larger scale in industry as shown in **Figure 9.1**

**Figure 9.1**

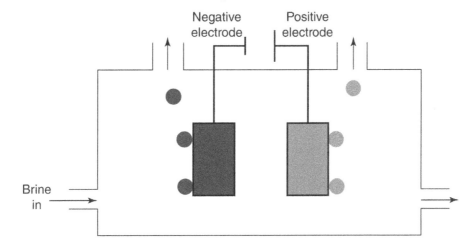

Complete **Table 9.1** to identify the name of the product left in the solution.

**Table 9.1**

| Location | Product |
|---|---|
| positive electrode | chlorine |
| negative electrode | hydrogen |
| product left in solution | |

[1 mark]

**Question 9 continues on the next page**

**09.3** Explain why hydrogen ions move to the negative electrode.

......................................................................................................................................

...................................................................................................................................... **[1 mark]**

**09.4** Explain why hydrogen forms at the negative electrode, but sodium does not.

......................................................................................................................................

...................................................................................................................................... **[1 mark]**

**09.5** Describe how a chloride ion turns into a chlorine atom.

......................................................................................................................................

...................................................................................................................................... **[1 mark]**

**09.6** Sodium chloride forms from the reaction between sodium and chlorine.

Balance the equation for this reaction, below.

$$\text{.......... } Na(s) + Cl_2(g) \rightarrow \text{.......... } NaCl(s)$$

**[1 mark]**

**09.7** Chlorine is in Group 7.

What is the name given to the elements in Group 7?

Tick **one** box.

Halogens ☐

Alkali metals ☐

Noble gases ☐

**[1 mark]**

©HarperCollins*Publishers* 2019

**09.8** **Table 9.2** provides information about the Group 7 elements.

**Table 9.2**

| Element | Colour in aqueous solution | Boiling point (°C) |
|---------|----------------------------|--------------------|
| fluorine | colourless | −185 |
| chlorine | green / yellow | |
| bromine | orange | 59 |
| iodine | | 184 |

Predict the colour of **iodine** in aqueous solution.

........................................................................................................................................... [1 mark]

**09.9** Predict the boiling point of **chlorine**.

........................................................................................................................................... [1 mark]

**09.10** When aqueous fluorine is added to lithium bromide solution, a displacement reaction occurs.

The equation for this reaction is:

$$2LiBr(aq) + F_2(aq) \rightarrow Br_2(aq) + 2LiF(aq)$$

Explain why a displacement reaction occurs.

........................................................................................................................................... [1 mark]

**09.11** What is the colour of the solution at the end of the reaction?

........................................................................................................................................... [1 mark]

**Turn over >**

**10** **Figure 10.1** shows **the outer shells of** beryllium and fluorine.

**Figure 10.1**

**10.1** Draw a diagram to show a **molecule** of fluorine, $F_2$

You only need to show the **outer** electron shells.

[1 mark]

**10.2** Beryllium reacts with fluorine to form beryllium fluoride.

Write down the empirical formula of beryllium fluoride.

_____ [1 mark]

©HarperCollins*Publishers* 2019

**10.3** Describe what happens
- when atoms of fluorine react with atoms of beryllium
- to the charge on any ions that form.

Use **Figure 10.1** to help you.

[4 marks]

**10.4** Fluorine is a gas at room temperature.

Beryllium fluoride is a solid at room temperature.

Explain why these two substances have these different properties.

You should include
- reference to the bonding involved
- a description of the structure of both fluorine and beryllium fluoride.

[6 marks]

**END OF QUESTIONS**

**BLANK PAGE**

©HarperCollins*Publishers* 2019

# Collins

# AQA
GCSE
# Chemistry

**F**

## SET B – Paper 2 Foundation Tier

Author: Paul Lewis

**Materials**

Time allowed: 1 hour 45 minutes

**For this paper you must have:**

- a ruler
- a calculator
- the Periodic Table (found on page 94).

**Instructions**

- Answer **all** questions in the spaces provided.
- Do all rough work in this book. Cross through any work you do not want to be marked.

**Information**

- There are 100 marks available on this paper.
- The marks for questions are shown in brackets.
- You are expected to use a calculator where appropriate.
- You are reminded of the need for good English and clear presentation in your answers.
- When answering questions 05.6 and 08.3 you need to make sure that your answer:
  - is clear, logical, sensibly structured
  - fully meets the requirements of the question
  - shows that each separate point or step supports the overall answer.

**Advice**

- In all calculations, show clearly how you work out your answer.

**Name:** ........................................................................................................................................

**01**  The foods we eat often contain additional food colourings.

**01.1**  Why do foods contain colourings?

Tick **one** box.

To improve the taste ☐

To make food look more appealing ☐

To make the food last longer ☐

To make the food smell better ☐

**[1 mark]**

**01.2**  A scientist analysed a food sample, Z, to check for the presence of additives.

This is the method used:

1.  Draw a baseline.

2.  Place a dot of each additive on the start line.

3.  Place a dot of Z on the start line.

4.  Place the bottom of the paper in a solvent and wait for 5 minutes.

**Figure 1.1** shows the result.

**Figure 1.1**

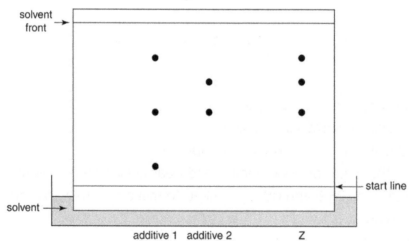

Name the analysis process used by the scientist.

Tick **one** box.

Chromatography ☐

Distillation ☐

Evaporation ☐

**[1 mark]**

©HarperCollins*Publishers* 2019

**01.3** The method outlined above does not include some important details about the start line and solvent level.

Suggest **two** improvements to the method.

1. ......................................................................................................................................

2. ...................................................................................................................... **[2 marks]**


**01.4** How many additives are in sample Z?

Use **Figure 1.1** to help you.

Tick **one** box.

2 ☐

3 ☐

4 ☐

7 ☐

**[1 mark]**

**Question 1 continues on the next page**

**01.5** Describe the differences between the dyes used in additive 1 and additive 2

........................................................................................................................................................

........................................................................................................................................................

........................................................................................................................................................

........................................................................................................................................................ **[2 marks]**

**01.6** Calculate the $R_f$ value for the dye that has travelled the furthest in additive 1

Use **Figure 1.1** and the equation:

$$R_f = \frac{\text{distance travelled by dye spot}}{\text{distance travelled by solvent front}}$$

Give your answer to 3 significant figures.

Distance travelled by dye spot = .............................................................................

Distance from start line to solvent front = ...............................................................

$R_f$ value = ...................................................................................................................

........................................................................................................................................................ **[5 marks]**

**02.1** **Figure 2.1** is a pie chart showing the composition of our **current** atmosphere.

**Figure 2.1**

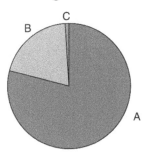

Which substance is represented by segment A?

Tick **one** box.

Oxygen ☐

Carbon dioxide ☐

Nitrogen ☐

Hydrogen ☐

[1 mark]

**02.2** What percentage of our current atmosphere is made up of **carbon dioxide**?

Tick **one** box.

>1% ☐

20% ☐

79% ☐

33% ☐

[1 mark]

**Question 2 continues on the next page**

**02.3** The amount of carbon dioxide and other greenhouse gases emitted over the life cycle of a product, service or event is called a *carbon footprint*.

State **two** ways in which we can reduce our carbon footprint.

1. ........................................................................................................................

2. ........................................................................................................  **[2 marks]**


**02.4** It is thought that, when Earth was first formed, carbon dioxide made up more than 95% of the atmosphere.

Carbon dioxide levels are much lower than that level now, because it can be removed from our atmosphere in various ways.

Describe what happened to reduce the high levels of carbon dioxide present in Earth's early atmosphere.

Use your own knowledge, and **Figure 2.2**, to help you.

**Figure 2.2**

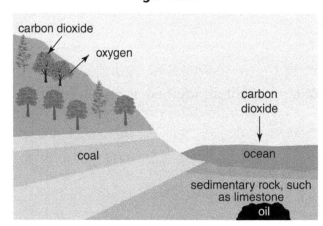

........................................................................................................................

........................................................................................................................

........................................................................................................................

........................................................................................................  **[3 marks]**

  ©HarperCollins*Publishers* 2019

**03** A group of students were carrying out the thermal decomposition of hydrated copper sulfate. In the reaction, hydrated copper sulfate, anhydrous copper sulfate and water are produced.

$$\text{hydrated copper sulfate} \rightleftharpoons \text{anhydrous copper sulfate} + \text{water}$$
$$\text{(blue)} \qquad\qquad\qquad \text{(white)}$$

**03.1** What does the $\rightleftharpoons$ symbol mean?

.................................................................................................................... **[1 mark]**

**03.2** What happens to the colour of copper sulfate when water is added to anhydrous copper sulfate?

.................................................................................................................... **[1 mark]**

**03.3** When the hydrated copper sulfate decomposes it takes in energy.

It is an **endothermic** reaction.

Name the type of reaction that occurs when anhydrous copper sulfate reacts with water.

.................................................................................................................... **[1 mark]**

**03.4** The students misplaced their container of copper sulfate. They decided to carry out some chemical tests on the substance they *thought* was copper sulfate.

Copper sulfate consists of copper(II) ions and sulfate ions.

The students carried out three tests, two of which were to try to identify copper(II) ions:

1. flame test
2. sodium hydroxide test
3. sulfate test

Identify the colour of the flame that the students would have seen when placing the substance in a flame, if copper(II) ions were present.

Tick **one** box.

Green ☐

Lilac ☐

Crimson ☐

Yellow ☐

**[1 mark]**

**Question 3 continues on the next page**

**03.5** Identify the result that the students would have seen when using sodium hydroxide solution to test if copper(II) ions were present.

Tick **one** box.

Blue precipitate ☐

Lilac precipitate ☐

Crimson precipitate ☐

Yellow precipitate ☐

**[1 mark]**

**03.6** Describe how to carry out the test for sulfates.

Include the name of any chemicals you would need.

State the result you would expect to see if sulfate ions were present.

Method _____

_____

_____

Result if sulfate ions are present _____

_____ **[3 marks]**

**03.7** Copper sulfate is used in formulations that increase copper levels in soil. It is used in fungicides, amongst other things.

Describe what is meant by the term *formulation*.

Explain why substances like this must be formulated.

_____

_____

_____ **[2 marks]**

©HarperCollins*Publishers* 2019

**04** Pure iron is soft and bends easily, and is not very useful.

**04.1** In science, what does the term *pure substance* mean?

.................................................................................................................................................. **[1 mark]**


**04.2** Pure iron is alloyed with other metals to make steel, which is more useful.

There are different types of steel depending on which other substances are added, and how much of each substance is added.

**Table 4.1** shows the composition of the formulations of different steels.

**Table 4.1**

| Type of steel | Percentage of metals (%) | | | |
|---|---|---|---|---|
| | iron | carbon | chromium | nickel |
| low carbon | 99.70 | 0.30 | – | – |
| medium carbon | 99.40 | 0.60 | – | – |
| high carbon | 98.85 | 1.15 | – | – |
| stainless austenitic | 73.20 | 0.80 | 18.00 | 8.00 |
| stainless ferritic | | 0.10 | 15.00 | 0.05 |
| stainless martensitic | 83.40 | 1.20 | 15.00 | 0.40 |

How much **iron** is in stainless ferritic steel?

.................................................................................................................................................. **[1 mark]**


**04.3** Explain why metal alloys are much **harder** than pure metals.

..................................................................................................................................................

..................................................................................................................................................

..................................................................................................................................................

.................................................................................................................................................. **[2 marks]**


**Question 4 continues on the next page**

**04.4** Draw **one** line from each type of steel to its use.

| Type of steel | Use |
|---|---|
| | jewellery |
| low carbon steel | cutlery |
| gold alloy | car body parts |
| high carbon steel | cutting tools |
| stainless steel | jet planes |
| | lunchboxes |

**[3 marks]**

**04.5** Substances such as fertilisers are also formulated products.

The Haber process is used to produce fertilisers.

In the Haber process, nitrogen and hydrogen react to form ammonia.

Balance the equation for the Haber process, below.

$$N_2 \text{ (g)} + \text{_____} H_2 \text{ (g)} \rightleftharpoons \text{_____} NH_3 \text{ (g)}$$

**[1 mark]**

**04.6** To achieve a high yield, this reaction has to happen at a specific temperature and pressure.

State the temperature and pressure that will achieve the maximum yield.

Temperature = _____ °C

Pressure = _____ atmospheres

**[2 marks]**

©HarperCollins*Publishers* 2019

**05** Crude oil is separated by fractional distillation to give products such as bitumen, diesel, petrol and LPG.

**Figure 5.1** is a diagram of a fractional distillation column.

**Figure 5.1**

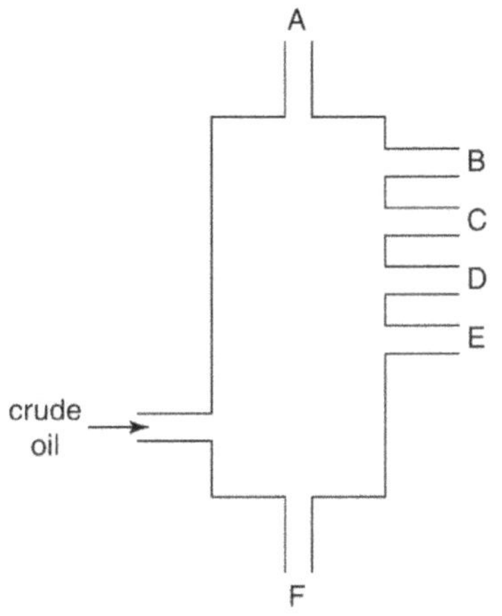

Fractional distillation allows for crude oil to be turned into useful substances.

**Table 5.1** shows information about some of the useful fractions that are produced in this process.

**Table 5.1**

| Fraction | Number of carbon atoms in the chain of the molecule | Boiling point (°C) |
|---|---|---|
| bitumen | 70< | 500–700 |
| fuel oil | 22–70 | 350–450 |
| diesel | 17–22 | 220–350 |
| kerosene | 10–16 | 160–220 |
| gasoline | 6–10 | 35–160 |
| LPG | 1–5 | <35 |

**Question 5 continues on the next page**

**05.1** Describe the steps involved in the process of fractional distillation of crude oil.

.......................................................................................................

.......................................................................................................

.......................................................................................................

.......................................................................................................

.......................................................................................................

.......................................................................................................

.......................................................................................................

.......................................................................................................

**[4 marks]**

**05.2** Using **Table 5.1 and Figure 5.1,** which letter on **Figure 5.1** represents where **LPG** is most likely to be produced?

Letter: ................................................ **[1 mark]**

**05.3** Using **Table 5.1 and Figure 5.1,** which letter on **Figure 5.1** represents where **diesel** is most likely to be produced?

Letter: ................................................ **[1 mark]**

**05.4** Describe the pattern in the data between **length of carbon chain** and **boiling point of each fraction**.

Use **Table 5.1** to help you.

.......................................................................................................

**[1 mark]**

©HarperCollins*Publishers* 2019

**05.5** Explain why each fraction has a range for their boiling point and not an exact temperature.

......................................................................................................................................................

......................................................................................................................................................

**[1 mark]**

**05.6** Many of the substances produced in fractional distillation can be used as fuels.

When fuels burn, it often impacts on the environment.

Fuels often contain combinations of hydrogen, carbon, sulfur and oxygen.

Describe the conditions in which different pollutants are formed.

Describe the impact the formed pollutants can have on the atmosphere.

......................................................................................................................................................

......................................................................................................................................................

......................................................................................................................................................

......................................................................................................................................................

......................................................................................................................................................

......................................................................................................................................................

......................................................................................................................................................

......................................................................................................................................................

......................................................................................................................................................

......................................................................................................................................................

......................................................................................................................................................

......................................................................................................................................................

......................................................................................................................................................

......................................................................................................................................................

**[6 marks]**

**Turn over >**

**06**   A student is investigating how temperature affects the rate of a reaction.

She is investigating how the temperature of 1 mol/dm³ hydrochloric acid affects how quickly a strip of magnesium reacts.

This is her method:

1. Place 25 cm³ of 20 °C 1 g/dm³ hydrochloric acid into a test tube.

2. Using scissors and a ruler, cut a 2 cm strip of magnesium.

3. Place the 2 cm strip of magnesium into the test tube with the acid. Start the timer.

4. When the magnesium is fully reacted, stop the timer.

5. Repeat steps 1–4 using different temperatures of 1 g/dm³ hydrochloric acid.

6. Repeat the investigation so you have three sets of results for each temperature.

**06.1**  Identify **two** control variables in this investigation.

1. ...................................................................................................................................................

2. ........................................................................................................................  **[2 marks]**

**06.2**  One source of inaccuracy in this experiment is the length of the magnesium strip.

Suggest an alternative method that would help overcome this.

.............................................................................................................................................

.........................................................................................................................  **[1 mark]**

                                                       ©HarperCollins*Publishers* 2019

**06.3** The student's results are shown in **Table 6.1**

**Table 6.1**

| Temperature of 1 g/dm³ hydrochloric acid (°C) | Time taken for the magnesium to react (s) | | | Mean time taken for the magnesium to react (s) |
|---|---|---|---|---|
| 20 | 73 | 73 | 76 | 74 |
| 30 | 70 | 60 | 57 | |
| 40 | 37 | 33 | 36 | 35 |
| 50 | 24 | 26 | 24 | 25 |
| 60 | 14 | 16 | 13 | 14 |

Calculate the mean for the set of results at 30 °C

......................................................................................................................

......................................................................................................................

Mean = ................................ s  **[2 marks]**

**Question 6 continues on the next page**

**06.4** Plot these results on the grid below.

Draw a line of best fit.

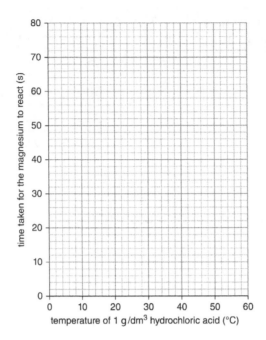

[3 marks]

**06.5** Give a conclusion about how temperature affects the rate of a reaction.

Use your graph to help you.

Use collision theory to help explain your conclusion.

_____

_____

_____

_____

_____

[3 marks]

©HarperCollins*Publishers* 2019

**07** This question is about alkanes, alkenes and polymers.

**Compound A**

$$H-\underset{\underset{H}{|}}{\overset{\overset{H}{|}}{C}}-\underset{\underset{H}{|}}{\overset{\overset{H}{|}}{C}}-\underset{\underset{H}{|}}{\overset{\overset{H}{|}}{C}}-H$$

**07.1** What is the formula of **Compound A**?

_____ **[1 mark]**

**07.2** State the chemical name of **Compound A**.

_____ **[1 mark]**

**07.3** Draw the structure of an **alkene** with the same number of carbons as **Compound A**.

**[1 mark]**

**07.4** Long alkanes can be decomposed into shorter alkanes by the process of **cracking**.

Give **two** methods of cracking that can be used.

1. _____

2. _____ **[2 marks]**

**Question 7 continues on the next page**

**07.5** Describe a chemical test to show whether a product of cracking is **unsaturated**.

Describe the result you would expect.

Test ................................................................................................................................

................................................................................................................................

Result ...........................................................................................................................

................................................................................................................................ **[2 marks]**


**07.6** Ethene has the formula $C_2H_4$

We can use ethene to make poly(ethene), which is used in everyday life.

Complete the equation below to show the formation of poly(ethene) from ethene.

$$n \quad \begin{array}{c} H \quad\; H \\ |\qquad| \\ C = C \\ |\qquad| \\ H \quad\; H \end{array} \longrightarrow$$

**[3 marks]**

©HarperCollins*Publishers* 2019

08    Many objects are made from **finite resources**.

08.1  What is meant by the term *finite resource*?

_____ **[1 mark]**


08.2  Identify **two** ways that we can prevent waste in the use of resources.

Tick **two** boxes.

Resource is sent to landfill          ☐

Resource is recycled                  ☐

Resource is sent for incineration     ☐

Resource is reused                    ☐

**[2 marks]**


08.3  Limestone and copper are both finite resources that can be used to make statues.

**Table 8.1** gives some information about these materials.

**Table 8.1**

|  | Limestone | Copper |
|---|---|---|
| **Extracting processes** | quarrying and powdering | mining, reduction, electrolysis and alloying |
| **Availability of raw material** | readily available | rapidly reducing |
| **Energy required to produce 1 kg of the substance** | 2.5 kWh | 22.5 kWh |
| **Can it be recycled?** | no specific recycling systems in place; less than 5% is recycled | recycled more than any other metal used in engineering; 45% of all copper used is from recycled copper |
| **Resistant to corrosion?** | corrodes in areas where rain is more acidic | resistant; very unreactive |
| **Average cost per kg** | £2.75 | £4.25 |


**Question 8 continues on the next page**

Write a life cycle assessment to compare the use of limestone and copper for making statues.

[6 marks]

©HarperCollins*Publishers* 2019

09.1 For river water to be safe for human consumption, the water needs to be treated to make it potable.

Figure 9.1 shows the stages that river water goes through to be made potable.

**Figure 9.1**

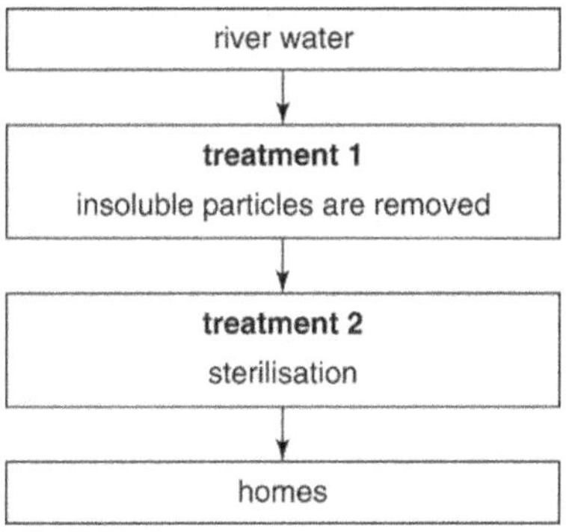

What is the name given to the process used in **Treatment 1**?

............................................................................................................................................................ [1 mark]

09.2 Water is sterilised in **Treatment 2** to kill any microbes that could make humans ill.

Which process is used during sterilisation?

Tick **one** box.

Adding hydrogen ☐

Neutralisation ☐

Using ultraviolet light ☐

Using microwaves ☐

[1 mark]

09.3 Another way to sterilise water is to use chlorine.

Describe the chemical test for identifying **chlorine gas**.

Describe the result you would expect.

Test ...............................................................................................................................................

............................................................................................................................................................

Result ...............................................................................................................................................

............................................................................................................................................................ [2 marks]

**Question 9 continues on the next page**

**09.4** **Table 9.1** shows the results of tests carried out on three unknown solutions.

Table 9.1

| Solution | Flame test | Test and result | | |
| --- | --- | --- | --- | --- |
| | | Sodium hydroxide solution | Barium chloride solution and acid added | Hydrochloric acid added; delivery tube connected to limewater |
| X | lilac | – | – | limewater turned cloudy |
| Y | – | brown precipitate | white precipitate | – |
| Z | – | white precipitate which dissolves in excess sodium hydroxide and goes colourless | – | – |

Identify X and Y and the metal ion in Z.

Solution X is ........................................

Solution Y is ........................................

Metal ion in Z is ........................................ **[5 marks]**

**09.5** Elements and compounds can also be identified using instrumental methods.

Suggest **one** way that instrumental methods are better than more traditional methods.

........................................................................................................ **[1 mark]**

©HarperCollins*Publishers* 2019

**10.1** Alkenes are a family of hydrocarbons with many uses. They undergo many reactions.

What is meant by the term *hydrocarbon*?

_____

_____ [2 marks]

**10.2** Complete the equation below to show the product which forms in the reaction between butene $C_4H_8$ and steam $H_2O$.

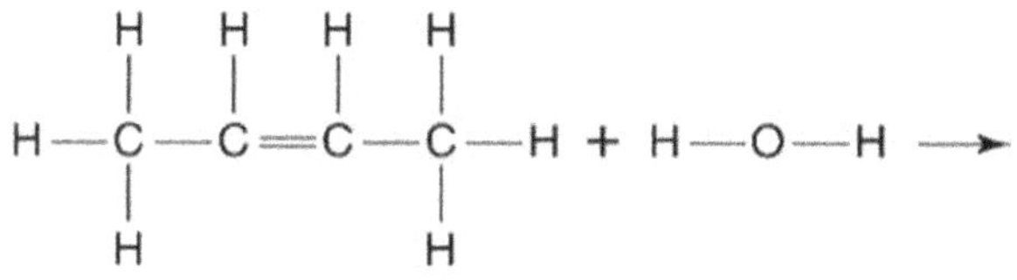

[2 marks]

**10.3** What is the functional group that alcohols contain?

_____ [1 mark]

**10.4** Propanoic acid is a carboxylic acid which can be made from propanol and one other reactant.

Name the other reactant.

State the type of reaction.

Reactant _____

Type of reaction _____ [2 marks]

**END OF QUESTIONS**

# The Periodic Table

## Key

Metals

Non-metals

**Relative atomic mass** — 1
**Atomic symbol** — **H**
**Name** — hydrogen
**Atomic/proton number** — 1

| 1 | 2 | | | | | | | | | | | | 3 | 4 | 5 | 6 | 7 | 0 or 8 |
|---|---|---|---|---|---|---|---|---|---|---|---|---|---|---|---|---|---|---|
| | | | | | | | | | | | | | | | | | | 4 **He** helium 2 |
| 7 **Li** lithium 3 | 9 **Be** beryllium 4 | | | | | | | | | | | | 11 **B** boron 5 | 12 **C** carbon 6 | 14 **N** nitrogen 7 | 16 **O** oxygen 8 | 19 **F** fluorine 9 | 20 **Ne** neon 10 |
| 23 **Na** sodium 11 | 24 **Mg** magnesium 12 | | | | | | | | | | | | 27 **Al** aluminium 13 | 28 **Si** silicon 14 | 31 **P** phosphorus 15 | 32 **S** sulfur 16 | 35.5 **Cl** chlorine 17 | 40 **Ar** argon 18 |
| 39 **K** potassium 19 | 40 **Ca** calcium 20 | 45 **Sc** scandium 21 | 48 **Ti** titanium 22 | 51 **V** vanadium 23 | 52 **Cr** chromium 24 | 55 **Mn** manganese 25 | 56 **Fe** iron 26 | 59 **Co** cobalt 27 | 59 **Ni** nickel 28 | 63.5 **Cu** copper 29 | 65 **Zn** zinc 30 | | 70 **Ga** gallium 31 | 73 **Ge** germanium 32 | 75 **As** arsenic 33 | 79 **Se** selenium 34 | 80 **Br** bromine 35 | 84 **Kr** krypton 36 |
| 85 **Rb** rubidium 37 | 88 **Sr** strontium 38 | 89 **Y** yttrium 39 | 91 **Zr** zirconium 40 | 93 **Nb** niobium 41 | 96 **Mo** molybdenum 42 | [98] **Tc** technetium 43 | 101 **Ru** ruthenium 44 | 103 **Rh** rhodium 45 | 106 **Pd** palladium 46 | 108 **Ag** silver 47 | 112 **Cd** cadmium 48 | | 115 **In** indium 49 | 119 **Sn** tin 50 | 122 **Sb** antimony 51 | 128 **Te** tellurium 52 | 127 **I** iodine 53 | 131 **Xe** xenon 54 |
| 133 **Cs** caesium 55 | 137 **Ba** barium 56 | 139 **La\*** lanthanum 57 | 178 **Hf** hafnium 72 | 181 **Ta** tantalum 73 | 184 **W** tungsten 74 | 186 **Re** rhenium 75 | 190 **Os** osmium 76 | 192 **Ir** iridium 77 | 195 **Pt** platinum 78 | 197 **Au** gold 79 | 201 **Hg** mercury 80 | | 204 **Tl** thallium 81 | 207 **Pb** lead 82 | 209 **Bi** bismuth 83 | [209] **Po** polonium 84 | [210] **At** astatine 85 | [222] **Rn** radon 86 |
| [223] **Fr** francium 87 | [226] **Ra** radium 88 | [227] **Ac\*** actinium 89 | [261] **Rf** rutherfordium 104 | [262] **Db** dubnium 105 | [266] **Sg** seaborgium 106 | [264] **Bh** bohrium 107 | [277] **Hs** hassium 108 | [268] **Mt** meitnerium 109 | [271] **Ds** darmstadtium 110 | [272] **Rg** roentgenium 111 | [285] **Cn** copernicium 112 | | [286] **Uut** ununtrium 113 | [289] **Fl** flerovium 114 | [289] **Uup** ununpentium 115 | [293] **Lv** livermorium 116 | [294] **Uus** ununseptium 117 | [294] **Uuo** ununoctium 118 |

*The lanthanides (atomic numbers 58–71) and the actinides (atomic numbers 90–103) have been omitted.
The relative atomic masses of copper and chlorine have not been rounded to the nearest whole number.

©HarperCollinsPublishers 2019

# Answers

## Set A – Paper 1

| Question | Answer(s) | Extra info | Mark(s) | AO/Spec ref. |
|---|---|---|---|---|
| 01.1 | The top right corner contains non-metals only. | | 1 | AO1 4.1.2.1 |
| 01.2 | have a full outer shell of electrons | | 1 | AO1 4.1.2.4 |
| 01.3 | Group 7 elements have seven electrons in the outer most shell. | | 1 | AO1 4.1.2.6 |
| | Group 7 elements form both ionic compounds and covalent molecules. | | 1 | |
| 01.4 | Reactivity increases / get more reactive | | 1 | AO1 4.1.2.5 |
| 01.5 | Reactivity decreases / get less reactive | | 1 | AO1 4.1.2.6 |
| 01.6 | Boiling points increase | | 1 | AO1 4.1.2.4 |
| 01.7 | any two from: higher melting points; higher boiling points; higher density; coloured compounds; stronger | | 2 | AO1 4.1.3.1 |
| 02.1 | magnesium sulfate | | 1 | AO2 4.4.2.2 |
| 02.2 | **Level 3**: A detailed and coherent comparison is given, which demonstrates a broad knowledge and understanding of the key scientific ideas. All processes are described and explained in logical order. Explanation for the processes are given. For example, excess magnesium oxide is added to make sure all the acid is reacted, or the solution is heated to evaporate and remove most of the water. | | 5–6 | AO3 4.4.2.3 |
| | **Level 2**: A description is given which demonstrates a reasonable knowledge and understanding of the key scientific ideas. The method is logical and the processes followed will produce salt solution. The processes of heating, filtration, evaporation and crystallisation are described in order. | | 3–4 | |
| | **Level 1**: Demonstrates a basic knowledge of some of the relevant ideas. Key appropriate equipment are named correctly. Most of the main processes are present, but may not be in logical order. For example, evaporation may be placed before filtration. | | 1–2 | |
| | **No relevant content** | | 0 | |

| Question | Answer(s) | Extra info | Mark(s) | AO/Spec ref. |
|---|---|---|---|---|
| | **Indicative content** <br>• Add an appropriate volume of sulfuric acid (10 to 30 cm³) to a beaker. Precise measurement of the acid is not required. <br>• Heat the acid in a water bath to speed up the reaction. Limit the temperature to 40°C as acid is corrosive. <br>• Add small amounts of magnesium oxide to the beaker and stir, until the magnesium oxide is seen to dissolve. <br>• When there is excess insoluble magnesium oxide remaining, cool the beaker. <br>• Filter the solution into a clean evaporating dish, with a funnel and filter paper. This removes any insoluble magnesium oxide. <br>• Heat the evaporating dish on a tripod using a Bunsen burner, or in a water bath set to about 70°C, until about third of the solution remains. <br>• Allow the dish to cool, so that crystals can form. <br>• Dry the crystals between the folds of filter paper to remove any remaining water. | | | |
| 02.3 | bubbles / effervescence / evidence of hydrogen released | | 1 | AO2 4.4.2.2 |
| 02.4 | Measure the initial and maximum temperature of the sulfuric acid using a thermometer. | | 1 | AO3 4.5.1.1 |
| 02.5 | (in order) magnesium, zinc, iron, copper (2 marks for all four in correct order; 1 mark for two or three in correct order) | | 2 | AO3 4.4.1.2 4.5.1.1 |
| 03.1 | Nanoparticles have a diameter less than 2500 nm. | | 1 | AO1 4.2.4.1 |
| 03.2 | New jewellery | | 1 | AO1 4.2.4.2 |
| 03.3 | buckminster-fullerene, diamond, graphite, graphene (3 marks for all four in correct order; 2 marks for two correct or 1 mark for one correct) | | 3 | AO1 4.2.3.1 4.2.3.2 4.2.3.3 |

| Question | Answer(s) | Extra info | Mark(s) | AO/Spec ref. |
|---|---|---|---|---|
| 03.4 | They are made from carbon atoms only. | | 1 | AO2 4.2.3.1 4.2.3.2 4.2.3.3 |
| | The atoms are joined by covalent bonds. | | 1 | |
| 03.5 | all solids (except mercury) at room temperature | | 1 | AO2 4.2.2.7 4.2.2.3 |
| | high melting / boiling points | | 1 | |
| | conduct electricity when molten | | 1 | |
| 03.6 | Similarities: | | 5 | AO2 4.2.3.2 4.2.3.1 |
| | both made from C atoms only | | | |
| | strong covalent bonds between C atoms | | | |
| | giant covalent structure | | | |
| | Differences: | | | |
| | graphite has delocalised electrons; diamond does not | | | |
| | graphite has weak intermolecular forces between layers; diamond does not form layers | | | |
| 04.1 | sodium + oxygen → sodium oxide | | 1 | AO2 4.1.1.1 |
| 04.2 | Oxidation | | 1 | AO2 4.4.1.1 |
| 04.3 | It will increase | | 1 | AO2 4.4.1.1 4.3.1.1 |
| 04.4 | Na transfers one electron to form $Na^+$ | | 1 | AO2 4.2.1.2 |
| | O gains two electrons to form $O^{2-}$ | | 1 | |
| | Therefore, two Na atoms react with one O atom… | | 1 | |
| | …and therefore the formula is $Na_2O$ | | 1 | |
| 04.5 | $4Na + O_2 → 2Na_2O$ | | 1 | AO2 4.1.1.1 |
| 04.6 | $55 ÷ 62 × 100 = 88.7\%$ | | 1 | AO2 4.3.3.1 |
| 04.7 | 100% | | 1 | AO3 4.3.3.2 |
| | because there are no other products | | 1 | |
| 04.8 | $Na_2CO_3 → Na_2O + CO_2$ | | 1 | AO2 4.1.1.1 |
| 04.9 | It will decrease | | 1 | AO1 4.3.1.3 |
| 04.10 | It will be lower | | 1 | AO2 4.3.3.2 |
| | because there is another product. | | 1 | |
| 05.1 | A = 10.5; B = −5.67; C = 25.5; D = −11.0 | | 4 | AO2 4.5.1.1 |
| 05.2 | random error | | 1 | AO1 4.5.1.1 |
| | not all the results are affected in the same way. | | 1 | |

| Question | Answer(s) | Extra info | Mark(s) | AO/Spec ref. |
|---|---|---|---|---|
| 05.3 | any three from: | | 3 | AO3 4.5.1.1 |
| | A and C are exothermic reactions. | | | |
| | B and D are endothermic reactions. | | | |
| | D is more endothermic than B. | | | |
| | C is more exothermic than A. | | | |
| | Allow any other conclusions consistent with the correct data. | | | |
| | Also allow ecf from miscalculation (or incorrect use of +/-) in 05.1 – as long as conclusion is consistent with data in 05.1. | | | |
| 05.4 | A = X; B = Y; C = X; D = Y | 2 marks for all four correct; 1 mark for three correct; no marks for one or two correct only | 2 | AO2 4.5.1.2 |
| | allow ecf from miscalculation (or incorrect use of +/-) | | | |
| 06.1 | potassium nitrate and water | | 1 | AO1 4.4.2.2 |
| 06.2 | 10 ÷ 40 | | 1 | AO2 4.3.2.5 |
| | = 0.25 g (in 25 cm³) | | 1 | |
| 06.3 | **Level 3**: A detailed and coherent comparison is given, which demonstrates a broad knowledge and understanding of the key scientific ideas. Precise information about filling burette with nitric acid; pipette to measure quantity of KOH solution; addition of indicator; care near end-point; repeat until consistent results obtained. | | 5–6 | AO2 4.4.2.5 |
| | **Level 2**: A description is given which demonstrates a reasonable knowledge and understanding of the key scientific ideas. Use of burette and pipette for measuring volumes, need for an indicator. | | 3–4 | |
| | **Level 1**: Demonstrates a basic knowledge of some of the relevant ideas. Simple statements are made, such as nitric acid is added to KOH solution until the colour changes; mention of need to measure volumes. | | 1–2 | |
| | **No relevant content** | | 0 | |

©HarperCollinsPublishers 2019

| Question | Answer(s) | Extra info | Mark(s) | AO/Spec ref. |
|---|---|---|---|---|
| | **Indicative content** <br>• Pour nitric acid in burette. <br>• Use a 25 cm³ pipette/measuring cylinder for KOH. <br>• Add a few drops of named indicator e.g. phenolphthalein. <br>• Correct colour change of indicator before and after neutralisation. <br>• Add nitric acid dropwise, until indicator just changes colour permanently. <br>• Record volume of nitric acid used. <br>• Repeat until results are consistent (to within 0.1 cm³). | | | |
| 07.1 | polystyrene, or any suitable insulator | | 1 | AO1 <br>4.5.1.1 |
| 07.2 | x-axis labelled 'volume', with units | | 1 | AO2 <br>4.4.2.2 <br>4.4.2.4 |
| | y-axis labelled 'temperature', with units | | 1 | |
| | suitable even scale for each axes | | 1 | |
| | points correctly plotted | | 1 | |
| 07.3 | lines of best fit correctly drawn | | 2 | AO2 <br>4.4.2.2 <br>4.4.2.4 |
| 07.4 | 20 cm³ | | 1 | AO3 <br>4.4.2.2 <br>4.4.2.4 |
| 07.5 | $H^+$ (aq) + $OH^-$ (aq) → $H_2O$ (l) | | 1 | AO1 <br>4.4.2.2 <br>4.4.2.4 |
| 07.6 | 10 cm³ — pH 2–4 | | 1 | AO2 <br>4.4.2.2 <br>4.4.2.4 |
| | 15 cm³ — pH 2–4 | | 1 | |
| | 25 cm³ — pH 10–12 | | 1 | |
| | 40 cm³ — pH 10–12 | | 1 | |
| 08.1 | | | 1 | AO1 <br>4.1.1.7 |
| 08.2 | | 1 mark for correct number of electrons; 1 mark for brackets and 2⁻ | 1 <br><br>1 | AO2 <br>4.1.1.7 |
| 08.3 | The radius of an atom is about 0.1 nm | | 1 | AO1 <br>4.1.1.5 |
| 08.4 | Isotopes contain the same number of protons. | | 1 | AO1 <br>4.1.1.5 |
| | Isotopes contain the same number of electrons. | | 1 | |

| Question | Answer(s) | Extra info | Mark(s) | AO/Spec ref. |
|---|---|---|---|---|
| 08.5 | Similarities: <br>All isotopes have 8 protons / 8 electrons / or they all have the same number of protons **and** the same number of electrons. | | 1 | AO1 <br>4.1.1.5 |
| | Differences: <br>They all have different number of neutrons. | | 1 | |
| 08.6 | (70 × 16) + (25 × 17) + (5 × 18) | | 1 | AO2 <br>4.1.1.6 |
| | ÷ 100 | | 1 | |
| | = 16.35 | | 1 | |
| 09.1 | The beam produced is deflected by an electric field. | | 1 | AO1 <br>4.1.1.3 |
| | Flashes of light were observed when particles hit the screen. | | 1 | |
| 09.2 | Evidence: <br>Most alpha particles passed straight through the gold foil. <br>A small proportion of alpha particles rebounded. | | 2 | AO3 <br>4.1.1.3 |
| | Explanation: <br>As most passed through, the atom must be made mostly of empty space. <br>Rebounding suggests the alpha particles hit a central **positive** nucleus. | | 2 | |

## Set A – Paper 2

| Question | Answer(s) | Extra info | Mark(s) | AO/Spec ref. |
|---|---|---|---|---|
| 01.1 | Oxygen from a cylinder | | 1 | AO2 <br>4.8.1.1 |
| 01.2 | Formulations must be pure substances in order to be safe. | | 1 | AO1 <br>4.8.1.1 <br>4.8.1.2 |
| 01.3 | (top to bottom) F, M, F, M | | 4 | AO1 <br>4.8.1.1 <br>4.8.1.2 |
| 01.4 | Oxygen | | 1 | AO1 <br>4.9.3.1 |
| 01.5 | carbon dioxide | | 1 | AO1 <br>4.9.2.2 |
| | methane | | 1 | |
| 02.1 | Methane, ethane, propane, butane | | 1 | AO1 <br>4.7.1.1 |
| 02.2 | Alkanes and alkenes are both part of a homologous series. | | 1 | AO1 <br>4.7.1.1 <br>4.7.2.1 |
| 02.3 | …they can flow less easily and are harder to pour. | | 1 | AO2 <br>4.7.1.3 |
| | …the boiling point increases. | | 1 | |
| 02.4 | | | 1 | AO2 <br>4.7.2.1 |

| Question | Answer(s) | Extra info | Mark(s) | AO/Spec ref. |
|---|---|---|---|---|
| 02.5 | (in order) mixture, boiling, evaporate, cool, condense | | 5 | **AO1** 4.7.1.2 |
| 03.1 | Alkanes and alkenes are both very reactive. | | 1 | **AO1** 4.7.2.2 4.7.2.3 4.7.2.4 |
| 03.2 | Propane | | 1 | **AO2** 4.7.2.2 |
| 03.3 | Steam cracking takes place at a higher temperature than catalytic cracking. | | 1 | **AO1** 4.7.1.4 |
| | More alkenes are produced in steam cracking than catalytic cracking. | | 1 | |
| 03.4 | add bromine water | | 1 | **AO2** 4.7.1.4 |
| | turns colourless with propene (but remains orange with propane) | | 1 | |
| 03.5 | $C_5H_{12}$ or $2C_4H_8 + CH_4$ | | 2 | **AO2** 4.7.1.4 |
| 03.6 | ethene | | 1 | **AO2** 4.7.2.3 |
| 03.7 | fermentation — low temperature and pressure AND anaerobic | | 1 | **AO1** 4.7.2.3 |
| | adding water to a hydrocarbon — high temperature and pressure AND addition of a metal catalyst | | 1 | |
| 04.1 | The rate of reaction is faster with a higher concentration. | | 1 | **AO1** 4.6.1.2 |
| 04.2 | m/s | | 1 | **AO2** 4.6.1.1 |
| 04.3 | Measure the total volume of hydrogen in the gas syringe and divide by the time taken to make it. | | 1 | **AO2** 4.6.1.1 |
| 04.4 | correctly plotted points | | 1 | **AO3** 4.6.1.1 |
| | correct line of best fit | | 1 | |
| | anomalous result highlighted (1; 100) | | 1 | |
| 04.5 | $900 \div 15$ = 60 (cm³/s) | 2 marks for correct value without working | 1 1 | **AO2** 4.6.1.1 |
| 04.6 | rate increases with increasing concentration | | 1 | **AO3** 4.6.1.2 |
| 04.7 | at a higher concentration, there are more particles | | 1 | **AO2** 4.6.1.3 |
| | reacting particles collide more frequently, so greater chance of collision being successful | | 1 | |

| Question | Answer(s) | Extra info | Mark(s) | AO/Spec ref. |
|---|---|---|---|---|
| 05.1 | hydrogen — insert burning splint; a pop sound is heard | | 1 | **AO1** 4.8.2.1 |
| | chlorine — place damp litmus into the gas; litmus will turn white | | 1 | 4.8.2.2 4.8.2.3 |
| | oxygen — insert glowing splint; splint will relight | | 1 | 4.8.2.4 |
| | carbon dioxide — bubble gas through limewater; limewater will turn cloudy | | 1 | |
| 05.2 | $Cu^{2+}$ | allow copper 2+ or copper(II) or copper, 2+ charge | 1 | **AO2** 4.8.3.2 |
| 05.3 | add barium chloride with hydrochloric acid | | 1 | **AO1** 4.8.3.5 |
| | a white precipitate is observed if sulfate ions are present | | 1 | |
| 05.4 | cation in salt A – lithium | | 1 | **AO2** 4.8.3.1 |
| | anion in salt A – bromide | | 1 | 4.8.3.2 |
| | cation in salt B – iron(III) | | 1 | 4.8.3.4 |
| | anion in salt B – sulfate | | 1 | 4.8.3.5 |
| 05.5 | more accurate | | 1 | **AO1** 4.8.3.6 |
| | more sensitive | | 1 | |
| | more rapid / faster / quicker | | 1 | |
| 05.6 | it is potassium (K)... | | 1 | **AO2** 4.8.3.7 |
| | ...the lines match / are in the same place as the spectra for K | | 1 | |
| 06.1 | any three from: | | 3 | **AO3** 4.9.1.1 |
| | more nitrogen in present atmosphere / no nitrogen in early atmosphere | | | |
| | more oxygen in present atmosphere / no oxygen in early atmosphere | | | |
| | more carbon dioxide in early atmosphere / less carbon dioxide in present atmosphere | | | |
| | small amounts of ammonia in early atmosphere / no ammonia in atmosphere today | | | |
| 06.2 | description **and** explanation required for each | | 4 | **AO2** 4.9.1.2 |
| | any two from: | | | 4.9.1.4 |
| | description: photosynthesis of green plants and algae explanation: $CO_2$ is taken in / absorbed so less $CO_2$ today | | | |
| | description: $CO_2$ dissolved in the oceans (producing carbonates) explanation: turned into limestone rock / locked away in limestone rock | | | |
| | description: $CO_2$ absorbed by plants which then decompose explanation: $CO_2$ is locked away in fossil fuels such as coal, crude oil and natural gas | | | |

©HarperCollins*Publishers* 2019

| Question | Answer(s) | Extra info | Mark(s) | AO/Spec ref. |
|---|---|---|---|---|
| 06.3 | $6CO_2 + 6H_2O \rightarrow C_6H_{12}O_6 + 6O_2$ | 1 mark for correct substances; 1 mark for correct balancing | 2 | AO1 4.9.1.3 |
| 06.4 | any two from: ice cap melt sea level rise climate change / more precipitation changes in biodiversity / extinctions loss of habitat (allow any other potential effects) | | 2 | AO2 4.9.2.3 |
| 06.5 | description **and** explanation required for each any four from: reduce the burning of fossil fuels, so less $CO_2$ is released reduce deforestation, so more $CO_2$ is absorbed reduce waste to landfill, so less methane is produced capture methane from landfill, so it doesn't enter the atmosphere reduce livestock farming, so less methane is produced increase energy efficiency, so less fossil fuels are burnt increase use of renewable fuels, so less fossil fuels are burnt (allow any other actions that would lead to a reduction in $CO_2$) | | 4 | AO2 4.9.2.3 4.9.2.4 |
| 07.1 | (both are safe to drink but) potable water contains dissolved substances / pure water does not contain any dissolved substances | | 1 | AO1 4.10.1.2 |
| 07.2 | River B three reasons (referring to choice and safety recommendations): less chloride than A **and** within safe limits less sodium than A **and** within safe limits pH higher than A **and** within safe limits | | 1  1  1  1 | AO3 4.10.1.2 |
| 07.3 | filtration sterilisation | | 1  1 | AO1 4.10.1.2 |
| 07.4 | to kill pathogens / to sterilise | | 2 | AO1 4.10.1.2 |

| Question | Answer(s) | Extra info | Mark(s) | AO/Spec ref. |
|---|---|---|---|---|
| 07.5 | **Level 3**: A detailed and coherent comparison is given, which demonstrates a broad knowledge and understanding of the key scientific ideas. The response makes logical links between the points raised and uses sufficient examples to support these links. | | 5–6 | AO3 4.10.1.2 |
| | **Level 2**: A description is given which demonstrates a reasonable knowledge and understanding of the key scientific ideas. Comparisons are made but may not be fully articulated and/or precise. | | 3–4 | |
| | **Level 1**: Simple statements are made which demonstrate a basic knowledge of some of the relevant ideas. The response may fail to make comparisons between the points raised. | | 1–2 | |
| | **No relevant content** | | 0 | |
| | **Indicative content** Both sources – sterilisation with one of ozone, chlorine or ultraviolet radiation **Seawater only** Desalination by distillation or reverse osmosis Large amounts of energy required Can only occur near a sea/ ocean Plentiful supply **Groundwater only** Needs to be pumped up from groundwater source Already naturally filtered through rock so extra filtration not needed May be contaminated with pesticides or fertilisers which need to be removed Limited supply – if overused may run out Overuse can lead to subsidence | | | |
| 08.1 | reaction is reversible | | 1 | AO1 4.6.2.1 |
| 08.2 | it is endothermic | | 1 | AO1 4.6.2.2 |
| 08.3 | 450 °C iron catalyst 200 atmospheres | | 1  1  1 | AO1 4.10.4.1 |
| 08.4 | ammonium hydroxide phosphoric acid | | 1  1 | AO2 4.10.4.2 |

| Question | Answer(s) | Extra info | Mark(s) | AO/Spec ref. |
|---|---|---|---|---|
| 08.5 | N = nitrogen, P = phosphorus, K = potassium | 1 mark for two correct; 2 marks for all three correct | 2 | **AO1**<br>4.10.4.2 |
| 08.6 | calcium phosphate + nitric acid → calcium nitrate + phosphoric acid | in each equation: 1 mark for products and 1 mark for reactants | 2 | **AO2**<br>4.10.4.2 |
| | phosphoric acid + ammonium hydroxide → ammonium phosphate + water | | 2 | |

©HarperCollins*Publishers* 2019

| Question | Answer(s) | Extra info | Mark(s) | AO/Spec ref. |
|---|---|---|---|---|
| 01.1 | Two elements in the same period = C and W | | 1 | AO1 |
| | An element with a full outer shell = Z or W | | 1 | 4.1.1.4 |
| | A transition metal = C | | 1 | 4.1.2.1 |
| | An element with only six protons = D | | 1 | 4.1.2.4 |
| | | | | 4.1.3.2 |
| 01.2 | 2,5 | | 1 | AO1 4.1.1.7 |
| 01.3 | 7 | | 1 | AO2 4.1.1.5 |
| 01.4 | Same number of protons and electrons | | 1 | AO2 |
| | Protons are positive and electrons are negative | | 1 | 4.1.1.4 |
| | (Opposite) Charges cancel each other out | | 1 | |
| 01.5 | element — a substance that is made from only one type of atom | | 1 | AO1 |
| | compound — where two or more substances have chemically combined | | | 4.1.1.1 |
| | mixture — where two or more substances are together but can be separated | | | 4.1.1.2 |
| | all have to be correct for one mark | | | |
| 02.1 | hydrogen | | 1 | AO1 4.1.1.1 |
| 02.2 | OH⁻ | allow hydroxide | 1 | AO2 4.4.2.4 |
| 02.3 | any two from: potassium... ...produces a lilac flame, sodium produces an orange flame ...fizzes / bubbles more...moves quicker across the surface ...melts / reacts faster | allow converse for each response | 2 | AO2 4.1.2.5 |

| Question | Answer(s) | Extra info | Mark(s) | AO/Spec ref. |
|---|---|---|---|---|
| 02.4 | any three from: • increasing size of atom / number of shells / atomic radius / more shells • increased shielding • outer electron / shell further from nucleus (must be talking about outer electrons)* • so less attraction for outer electron / shell • therefore outer electron lost more easily *It must be stated that we are talking about outer electrons here at some point during the response. However, there is no need for it to be repeated. If not then any marking point regarding electron should not be given. | allow converse arguments | 3 | AO2 4.1.2.5 |
| 02.5 | in the centre / middle | accept d-block accept another correct description of transition block location | 1 | AO1 4.1.3 |
| 02.6 | They are less reactive than Group 1 metals. | | 1 | AO1 4.1.3.1 |
| | They have higher melting points than Group 1 metals. | | 1 | |
| 03.1 | independent variable — type of metal dependent variable — number of bubbles control variable — concentration of acid used | all three correct for two marks, one or two correct for one mark | 2 | AO1 4.4.2.1 |
| 03.2 | gas syringe (allow 'syringe') | | 1 | AO1 4.6.1.2 |
| 03.3 | points correctly plotted | line must not include anomalous point | 1 | AO2 |
| | curve of best fit used to join points | | 1 | AO3 4.6.1.2 |

| Question | Answer(s) | Extra info | Mark(s) | AO/Spec ref. |
|---|---|---|---|---|
| 03.4 | 30 (seconds) | | 1 | AO3 |
| | the result doesn't follow the pattern / the result is less than 20 seconds | | 1 | 4.6.1.2 |
| 03.5 | Any two from: | | 2 | AO3 |
| | volume of hydrogen released was quick at first | | | 4.6.1.2 |
| | then slowed down over time. | | | |
| | reaction stopped at 50 seconds | | | |
| 03.6 | $23 \div 60$ | | 1 | AO2 |
| | = 0.4 (to 1 d.p.) | | 1 | 4.6.1.1 |
| 04.1 | Covalent | | 1 | AO1 |
| | | | | 4.2.1.4 |
| 04.2 | This substance is a giant covalent structure. — D | 5 correct = 4 marks | 4 | AO2 |
| | This substance is a compound. — A | 4 correct = 3 marks | | 4.2.2.1 |
| | This substance is a solid. — C | 3 correct = 2 marks | | 4.2.1.3 |
| | This substance is evaporating. — E | 2 correct = 1 mark | | 4.2.3.2 |
| | This substance is a gas. — B | 0 / 1 correct = 0 marks | | |
| 04.3 | Comparison (not just a description) of the features of the two models required: | | 4 | AO3 |
| | Plum pudding has electrons scattered or in random positions / nuclear model has electrons in shells/outside the nucleus. | | | 4.1.1.3 |
| | Plum pudding has no nucleus / nuclear model has a nucleus. | | | |
| | Plum pudding has no neutrons / nuclear model has neutrons in nucleus. | | | |
| | Plum pudding has a spread out positive charge/nuclear model has protons in a nucleus. | | | |
| 05.1 | calcium chloride = (+)9 °C | | 1 | AO3 |
| | potassium chloride = −6 °C | | 1 | 4.5.1.1 |
| 05.2 | | correct profile (reactants on LHS, products on RHS, and reactants higher than products) | 1 | AO3 |
| | | | | 4.5.1.1 |
| | | correct labels for reactants and products | 1 | |
| 05.3 | potassium chloride | | 1 | AO2 |
| | | | | 4.5.1.1 |
| 05.4 | exothermic | | 1 | AO1 |
| | | | | 4.5.1.1 |
| 05.5 | 111 | | 1 | AO2 |
| | | | | 4.3.1.2 |

| Question | Answer(s) | Extra info | Mark(s) | AO/Spec ref. |
|---|---|---|---|---|
| 06.1 | (in order): soft, distorted, harder | | 3 | AO1 |
| | | | | 4.2.2.7 |
| 06.2 | Diagram should show two electrons in the first shell, eight in the second and two in the third. | All shells must have the correct number of electrons for two marks; allow one mark for one error. | 2 | AO2 |
| | | | | 4.1.1.7 |
| 06.3 | 2 electrons in the outer shell, so Group 2 | | 1 | AO1 |
| | | | | 4.1.1.7 |
| | 3 electron shells, so Period 3 | | 1 | 4.1.2.1 |
| 06.4 | good conductors of electricity — delocalised electrons to carry a charge | 3 correct = 2 marks | 2 | AO1 |
| | | | | 4.2.1.5 |
| | | | | 4.2.2.7 |
| | often have a high melting points — strong electrostatic forces of attraction | 2 correct = 1 mark | | 4.2.2.8 |
| | malleable — have layers which can slide over each other | 0/1 correct = 0 marks | | |
| 06.5 | Their diameter is between 1–100 nm | accept 'their diameter is less than 100 nm.' | 1 | AO1 |
| | | | | 4.2.4.1 |
| 06.6 | $1.65 \times 10^{-1}$ nm | 1 mark for $16.5 \times 10^{-2}$ nm or $165 \times 10^{-3}$ nm | 2 | AO2 |
| | | | | 4.2.4.1 |
| 07.1 | 10.50 cm³ | | 1 | AO2 |
| | | | | 4.3.1.4 |
| 07.2 | mass of solute = $\frac{45}{1000} \times 10.5$ | | 1 | AO2 |
| | = 0.47 g | | 1 | 4.3.2.5 |
| 07.3 | 50.25 cm³ | allow no units | 1 | AO2 |
| | | | | 4.3.1.4 |
| 07.4 | sulfuric acid | | 1 | AO1 |
| | | | | 4.4.2.2 |
| 07.5 | neutralisation | | 1 | AO1 |
| | | | | 4.4.2.4 |
| 07.6 | **Level 3** Response contains a description that allows a successful titration to be completed. | | 5–6 | AO2 |
| | | | | 4.4.2.5 |
| | **Level 2** Response contains a reasonable description of an experimental method such as using the pipette/burette with given measurement, **or** the addition of the alkali to acid (or acid to alkali). | | 3–4 | |

©HarperCollinsPublishers 2019

| Question | Answer(s) | Extra info | Mark(s) | AO/Spec ref. |
|---|---|---|---|---|
| | **Level 1** Response only contains a weak description of how to use some of the equipment therefore having a weak method. | | 1–2 | |
| | **No indicative content** | | 0 | |
| | **Indicative content** <br> • volume of acid measured using pipette acid in (conical) flask <br> • putting indicator in acid / conical flask sodium hydroxide added to burette (below eye level) <br> • placing a white tile under flask for colour change to be seen more easily <br> • drop wise addition of alkali when near end point <br> • swirling motion used throughout <br> • colour change signifies end point <br> • record the volume of sodium hydroxide added | | | |
| 08.1 | carbon <br> three | | 1 <br> 1 | **AO1** <br> 4.2.3.2 <br> 4.2.3.3 |
| 08.2 | contains free / delocalised electrons… <br> …that can carry a charge (through the structure) | | 1 <br> 1 | **AO1** <br> 4.2.3.2 <br> 4.2.3.3 |
| 08.3 | (lubricants) contain graphite atoms that form in layers… <br> …which can slide over each other | | 1 <br> 1 | **AO1** <br> **AO2** <br> 4.2.3.2 |
| 09.1 | Molten magnesium chloride <br> A solution of potassium iodide | both answers needed for one mark; more than two ticks negates mark | 1 | **AO1** <br> 4.4.3.1 <br> 4.4.3.2 <br> 4.4.3.4 |
| 09.2 | sodium hydroxide | accept NaOH | 1 | **AO1** <br> 4.4.3.4 |
| 09.3 | Hydrogen ions are positive and opposite charges attract. | hydrogen ions are positive / opposite charges attract alone is not enough for the mark | 1 | **AO2** <br> 4.4.3.1 |
| 09.4 | Sodium is more reactive than hydrogen. (Sodium reacts with water to make sodium hydroxide; hydrogen does not react with water.) | accept converse | 1 | **AO2** <br> 4.4.1.2 <br> 4.4.3.1 <br> 4.4.3.4 |
| 09.5 | Chloride ion loses 1 electron. | | 1 | **AO2** <br> 4.2.1.4 |

| Question | Answer(s) | Extra info | Mark(s) | AO/Spec ref. |
|---|---|---|---|---|
| 09.6 | $2Na(s) + Cl_2(g) \rightarrow 2NaCl(s)$ | accept multiples (as long as remains balanced) | 1 | **AO2** <br> 4.3.1.1 |
| 09.7 | Halogens | | 1 | **AO1** <br> 4.1.2.6 |
| 09.8 | brown | accept dark red | 1 | **AO3** <br> 4.1.2.6 |
| 09.9 | −30 to −60 | | 1 | **AO3** <br> 4.1.2.6 |
| 09.10 | Fluorine is more reactive than bromine. | accept converse | 1 | **AO2** <br> 4.1.2.6 <br> 4.4.1.2 |
| 09.11 | orange | | 1 | **AO3** <br> 4.1.2.6 |
| 10.1 | both fluorines should have a further 6 electrons around its outer shell | accept dots and / or crosses to represent electrons | 1 | **AO2** <br> 4.1.1.7 <br> 4.2.1.4 |
| 10.2 | $BeF_2$ | | 1 | **AO2** <br> 4.2.1.2 <br> 4.2.1.3 |
| 10.3 | beryllium atom loses 2 electrons… <br> …and becomes an ion with a charge of 2+ <br> each fluorine atom gains 1 electron… <br> …resulting in 2 fluoride ions both with a charge of 1− | | 1 <br> 1 <br> 1 <br> 1 | **AO2** <br> 4.2.1.2 <br> 4.2.1.3 |
| 10.4 | **Level 3** There is a detailed response regarding the type of bonding and / or structure **and** melting / boiling point of beryllium fluoride **and** fluorine. Explanation of why fluorine is a gas at room temperature and beryllium fluoride is a solid. | | 5–6 | **AO2** <br> 4.2.1.2 <br> 4.2.1.3 <br> 4.2.1.4 <br> 4.2.2.3 <br> 4.2.2.4 |
| | **Level 2** There is a response regarding the type of bonding and / or structure **and** melting / boiling point of beryllium fluoride **or** fluorine. | | 3–4 | |
| | **Level 1** There is a simple comment / response regarding the type of bonding and / or structure **or** melting / boiling point of beryllium fluoride **or** fluorine. | | 1–2 | |
| | **No indicative content** | | 0 | |

©HarperCollins*Publishers* 2019

| Question | Answer(s) | Extra info | Mark(s) | AO/Spec ref. |
|---|---|---|---|---|
| | **Indicative content:** **Beryllium fluoride** • giant structure • ionic bonds **or** electrostatic attraction • strong bonds (in all directions) • between oppositely charged ions • solid at room temperature as large amounts of energy are needed to break bonds • this means it has a high melting point **Fluorine** • simple molecule / molecular structure • covalent bonds between atoms • weak intermolecular forces between molecules • (no/weak attraction / bonds between molecules) • forces are easily broken (by low levels of energy) • low boiling point • therefore a gas at room temperature | | | |

## Set B – Paper 2

| Question | Answer(s) | | Mark(s) | AO/Spec ref. |
|---|---|---|---|---|
| 01.1 | To make food look more appealing | | 1 | AO2 4.8.1.2 |
| 01.2 | chromatography | | 1 | AO1 4.8.1.3 |
| 01.3 | any two from: start line should be drawn in pencil water level must be below start line/colouring dots start line should be drawn with a ruler | | 2 | AO1 4.8.1.3 |
| 01.4 | 3 | | 1 | AO2 4.8.1.3 |
| 01.5 | any two from: additive 1 has three dyes additive 2 has two dyes additive 1 has two different dyes additives 1 and 2 have one dye that is the same | allow additive 1 has more dyes than additive 2 allow dyes, pigments, spots or colours | 2 | AO3 4.8.1.3 |

| Question | Answer(s) | | Mark(s) | AO/Spec ref. |
|---|---|---|---|---|
| 01.6 | Distance travelled by dye spot = 34 mm Distance from start line to solvent front = 43 mm 34 ÷ 43 = 0.7907 = 0.791 | allow values 32–36 allow values 41–45 allow ecf from table 0.791 with no working should be awarded 5 marks | 1 1 1 1 1 | AO2 4.8.1.3 |
| 02.1 | Nitrogen | | 1 | AO2 4.9.1.1 |
| 02.2 | >1% | | 1 | AO1 4.9.1.1 |
| 02.3 | any two from: burn / use less fossil fuels increase renewable energy use switch off electrical appliances ensure we have double glazing have your thermostat set low use low energy / more efficient appliances / light bulbs (allow any other sensible suggestion to reduce carbon footprint) | accept any suitable answer but both answers must be different; for example: 'walk to school' and 'use car less' are the same, so only 1 mark | 2 | AO1 4.9.2.4 |
| 02.4 | any three from: used for photosynthesis dissolves in oceans and seas locked up in limestone / carbonates locked up as a fossil fuel used by plants used to form shells | | 3 | AO1 4.9.1.4 |
| 03.1 | (it is a) reversible (reaction) | | 1 | AO1 4.6.2.1 |
| 03.2 | turns blue | | 1 | AO2 4.6.2.2 |
| 03.3 | exothermic | | 1 | AO1 4.6.2.2 |
| 03.4 | Green | | 1 | AO1 4.8.3.1 |
| 03.5 | Blue precipitate | | 1 | AO1 4.8.3.2 |

©HarperCollinsPublishers 2019

| Question | Answer(s) | | Mark(s) | AO/Spec ref. |
|---|---|---|---|---|
| 03.6 | Method: add barium chloride... | 'add acidified barium chloride' would gain both method marks | 1 | AO1 4.8.3.5 |
| | ...in the presence of dilute HCl | | 1 | |
| | Result: White precipitate | | 1 | |
| 03.7 | a mixture of chemicals that has been designed for a specific product... | or words to that effect | 1 | AO1 4.8.1.2 |
| | ...so that each tablet provides the same amount of active ingredient / is safe to use / produces predictable effects | | 1 | |
| 04.1 | a single element or compound (not mixed with anything else) | accept 100% one element or compound accept all one type of atom or molecule | 1 | AO1 4.8.1.1 |
| 04.2 | 84.85 | | 1 | AO2 4.10.3.2 |
| 04.3 | alloys have distorted layers | | 1 | AO1 4.2.2.7 |
| | therefore the layers cannot slide as easily | | 1 | |
| 04.4 | low carbon steel — car body parts, lunchboxes | 4 correct = 3 marks | 3 | AO2 4.10.3.2 |
| | gold alloy — jewellery | 3 correct = 2 marks | | |
| | high carbon steel — cutting tools | 2 correct = 1 mark | | |
| | stainless steel — cutlery | 0/1 correct = 0 marks | | |
| 04.5 | $N_2$ (g) + 3 $H_2$ (g) $\rightleftharpoons$ 2 $NH_3$ (g) | both numbers required | 1 | AO1 4.1.1.1 |
| 04.6 | Temperature = 450 °C | | 1 | AO1 4.10.4.1 |
| | Pressure = 200 atmospheres | | 1 | |
| 05.1 | any four from: | | 4 | AO2 4.7.1.2 |
| | crude oil is heated | | | |
| | most of the oil evaporates | | | |
| | vapours / gases (cool and) condense | | | |
| | at their own boiling point | | | |
| | substances that don't evaporate are tapped off at the bottom | | | |
| | substances that don't condense flow out of the top | | | |
| | (**must** be in this order as question asks for steps in the process) | | | |
| 05.2 | A | | 1 | AO2 4.7.1.2 |

| Question | Answer(s) | | Mark(s) | AO/Spec ref. |
|---|---|---|---|---|
| 05.3 | D | | 1 | AO2 4.7.1.3 |
| 05.4 | the longer the carbon chain length, the higher the boiling point of the fraction | | 1 | AO1 4.7.1.3 |
| 05.5 | each fraction is a mixture | accept 'fractions are not pure' | 1 | AO2 4.8.1.1 |
| 05.6 | **Level 3** Detailed response with statements regarding three types of pollution and their impact on the environment. | | 5–6 | AO1 4.9.2.1 4.9.3.1 4.9.3.2 |
| | **Level 2** Response contains statements about two types of pollution and links to their impact on the environment. | | 3–4 | |
| | **Level 1** Response is weak, with only a statement regarding a type of pollution or an impact of one type of pollution. | | 1–2 | |
| | **No indicative content** | | 0 | |
| | **Indicative content**<br>• carbon monoxide: incomplete combustion / insufficient oxygen to react with fuel; carbon monoxide gas is formed which is toxic<br>• carbon dioxide: complete combustion; greenhouse gas linked with global rise in temperatures<br>• carbon particles: incomplete combustion / insufficient oxygen to react with fuel; can cause global dimming, global dimming makes the Earth darker.<br>• oxides of nitrogen: at high temperatures in car engine, oxygen and nitrogen in the air react causing acid rain; acid rain can damage statues / wildlife<br>• sulfur and oxygen react to form acid rain; acid rain can damage statues / wildlife | | | |
| 06.1 | any two from: volume of acid concentration of acid length / size of magnesium | do not accept amount of magnesium | 2 | AO2 4.6.1.2 |
| 06.2 | use measuring apparatus with a higher resolution OR weigh the magnesium | | 1 | AO3 4.6.1.2 |
| 06.3 | ignore anomaly (70 s) | allow 59 for 2 marks | 1 | AO2 4.6.11 |
| | calculate mean (60 + 57 ÷ 2) = 58.5 | allow 62 or 62.3 for one mark | 1 | |

| Question | Answer(s) | | Mark(s) | AO/Spec ref. |
|---|---|---|---|---|
| 06.4 | all points plotted correctly | one error for 1 mark | 2 | AO1 4.6.1.2 |
| | line of best fit drawn correctly | no marks for more than one error | 1 | |
| 06.5 | as temperature increases, so does the rate of reaction | 1 mark for conclusion | 3 | AO2 4.6.1.3 |
| | any two from: | 2 marks for collision theory | | |
| | particles gain energy | ignore 'particles move more' | | |
| | they move faster | accept 'more chance of particle collision' | | |
| | more frequent and successful collisions | | | |
| 07.1 | $C_3H_8$ | numbers cannot be more than halfway up the letter | 1 | AO1 4.7.1.1 |
| 07.2 | propane | | 1 | AO1 4.7.1.1 |
| 07.3 | | | 1 | AO2 4.7.2.1 |
| 07.4 | high temperature | | 1 | AO1 4.7.1.4 |
| | catalyst or steam | | 1 | |
| 07.5 | Test: bromine water | | 1 | AO1 4.7.1.4 |
| | Result: bromine water turns colourless | | 1 | |
| 07.6 | | 1 mark for brackets | 3 | AO1 4.7.3.1 |
| | | 1 mark for single bond between carbon atoms | | |
| | | 1 mark for *n* and bonds leaving the brackets | | |
| 08.1 | a resource which will run out | or words to that effect | 1 | AO1 4.10.1.1 |
| 08.2 | Resource is recycled | each additional (wrong) tick negates 1 mark | 1 | AO1 4.10.2.2 |
| | Resource is reused | | 1 | |

| Question | Answer(s) | Mark(s) | AO/Spec ref. |
|---|---|---|---|
| 08.3 | **Level 3** An answer which contains some comparison of limestone and copper in the manufacture of statues. The answer should contain some consideration of extracting processes, availability of raw material, the energy required to produce 1 kg of the substance, whether it can be recycled, the substance's resistance to corrosion and the average cost. The answer should differentiate between quantifiable data and data requiring judgement. It should develop conclusions from the information given in the question. | 5–6 | AO3 4.10.2.1 4.10.2.2 |
| | **Level 2** An answer which contains some comparison of limestone and copper in the manufacture of statues. The answer should contain some consideration of extracting processes, availability of raw material, the energy required to produce 1 kg of the substance, whether it can be recycled, the substance's resistance to corrosion and the average cost, but may not be complete. | 3–4 | |
| | **Level 1** An answer which contains some relevant points, but does not draw conclusions from the data given. | 1–2 | |
| | **No relevant content** | 0 | |
| | **Indicative content** | | |
| | • Limestone only has two extracting processes. | | |
| | • Copper has four extracting processes. | | |
| | • Quarrying and mining can both create jobs and increase local economy. | | |
| | • Quarrying and mining also have negative aspects. | | |
| | • Lots of limestone available. | | |
| | • Running out of copper quickly, (phytomining/ bioleaching). | | |
| | • Limestone uses 1/10 of the energy compared to copper. | | |
| | • Only small amounts of limestone can be recycled in the end. | | |
| | • Lots of copper is recycled, so disposal will not waste resource. | | |
| | • Limestone is prone to corrosion, especially from acid rain. | | |
| | • Copper is very unreactive. | | |
| | • Limestone is cheaper than copper. | | |
| 09.1 | screening | accept filtration | 1 | AO1 4.10.1.2 |
| 09.2 | Using ultraviolet light | | 1 | AO1 4.10.1.2 |

©HarperCollinsPublishers 2019

| Question | Answer(s) | | Mark(s) | AO/Spec ref. |
|---|---|---|---|---|
| 09.3 | Test: use damp blue litmus (or any other pH indicator) paper | | 1 | **AO2**<br>4.8.2.4 |
| | Result: it bleaches | | 1 | |
| 09.4 | Solution X = potassium carbonate | 1 mark for potassium | 2 | **AO2**<br>4.8.3.1 |
| | | 1 mark for carbonate | | 4.8.3.2 |
| | Solution Y = iron(III) sulfate | | 2 | 4.8.3.3 |
| | | 1 mark for iron(III) | | 4.8.3.5 |
| | Metal ion in Z = aluminium | | 1 | |
| | | 1 mark for sulfate | | |
| 09.5 | any one from:<br>more rapid/quicker<br>more accurate<br>more sensitive | | 1 | **AO1**<br>4.8.3.6 |
| 10.1 | a compound made from hydrogen and carbon atoms... | | 1 | **AO1**<br>4.7.1.1 |
| | ...only | | 1 | |
| 10.2 | | 1 mark for single C–C bond | 2 | **AO2**<br>4.7.2.1 |
| | | 1 mark for addition of OH and H across double bond | | 4.7.2.2 |
| 10.3 | –OH / hydroxyl | | 1 | **AO1**<br>4.7.2.3 |
| 10.4 | Reactant: oxygen or oxidising agent | | 1 | **AO2**<br>4.7.2.4 |
| | Type of reaction: oxidation | | 1 | |

BLANK PAGE

©HarperCollins*Publishers* 2019

**BLANK PAGE**

**BLANK PAGE**

©HarperCollins*Publishers* 2019

**BLANK PAGE**

©HarperCollins*Publishers* 2019

**BLANK PAGE**

©HarperCollins*Publishers* 2019